THROUGH THE SEASONS BEFORE US

FOLLOWING NOTTINGHAM FOREST IN THE 80S

THROUGH THE SEASONS BEFORE US

FOLLOWING NOTTINGHAM FOREST IN THE 80S

Steve King

DB PUBLISHING

This edition published in Great Britain in 2013 by DB Publishing, an imprint of JMD Media.

Copyright © Steve King 2013

All Rights Reserved. No part of this publication may be reproduced, stored in a retrieval system, or transmitted in any form, or by any means, electronic, mechanical, photocopying, recording or otherwise without the prior permission in writing of the copyright holders, nor be otherwise circulated in any form or binding or cover other than in which it is published and without a similar condition being imposed on the subsequent publisher.

ISBN 9781780913391

Printed and bound by Copytech (UK) Limited, Peterborough.

CONTENTS

	PREFACE	7
1.	THATCHER'S KIDS	11
2.	THREE BECOMES FIVE	25
3.	THAT'S THE WAY TO DO IT	31
4.	THE BIG CITY	39
5.	ALL ABOARD	49
6.	WE'RE ENGLISH, WE'RE BARMY!	57
7.	ALL ABROAD	67
8.	FOREST BOYS WE ARE HERE!	79
9.	THE GREAT TRAIN ROBBERY	91
10.	DÉJÀ VU	109
11.	WHEN TWO TRIBES GO TO WAR	121
12.	72 HOURS LATER	133
13.	MORE THAN JUST A GAME	139
14.	NUMB	147
	FOOTNOTE	153

Preface

This book chronicles the true adventures of a group of football fans travelling to watch Nottingham Forest's controversial UEFA Cup Semi-Final Second Leg against Anderlecht back in 1984.

Their experiences mirrored those shared by fans of every football club in Britain at the time. All supporters from those years will relate to the excitement and incidents that arose on such football away days, back in the 1970's and early 1980's.

This was a time when football was the domain of the working class male; when football was a tribal culture that had long outgrown the confines of 90 minutes on a Saturday afternoon

Set against a backdrop of economic decline, deindustrialisation, urban decay and mass unemployment, football fans in Britain mirrored the brutal social climate of the era.

It was a time when football fans were treated like animals, herded to and from the grounds like cattle and given little or no respect from those who were policing them.

And if you treat people like animals, they will behave like animals.

The fans increasingly became the product of their environment, and in keeping with the competitive spirit that Maggie Thatcher had advocated since coming to power in 1979, going to the football had become dog eat dog... us versus them... the survival of the fittest.

By the early 1980's, football attendances had fallen to their lowest figures since the Second World War. Football hooliganism – or the 'English Disease' as it was being called – was blamed as the main cause for these ever-diminishing crowds.

The football authorities believed that it was killing the game. It was certainly costing them money, and money talks.

Football was left with little choice but to change its image in order to reverse its headlong decline in popularity.

The following 30 years witnessed an all-out war on football hooligans by the government, the police and the football authorities. The introduction of CCTV, banning orders, Police Football Intelligence Officers and draconian sentencing has combined to all but eliminate violence in and around the stadiums.

This in turn has led to a fundamental change in the type of people who make up the numbers in today's football crowds. The game safely attracts families into its grounds now, in numbers that were unimaginable 30 years ago.

On the pitch there have been many changes to the game's rules, primarily in an attempt to make the game more skilful and exciting to watch. But it has really been off the pitch where football has introduced the biggest catalogue of changes.

Notably there has been the formation of the Premier League, which re-branded the game and established a new elitist outlook by the top clubs.

There has been the adoption of all-seater stadiums – almost directly as a consequence of the Hillsborough disaster. This move away from the old-style terraces has transformed the atmosphere that surrounded and shaped football matches back in the early '80's.

In short, football has increasingly become Big Business. Every club has adopted an expansive corporate outlook, looking to maximise their potential revenue streams.

In accordance with this, increased marketing and sponsorship deals have followed, as well as a rise in admission prices. (In 1982, entry to league matches featuring the top English teams cost as little as £3, yet by 2012 some clubs are charging over £50.)

The most significant factor in the changing public face of football can be attributed to the massive impact made by Sky television's influence.

Their money has enabled half-decent players to become multi-millionaires – whilst forcing fans to endure their traditional Saturday afternoon entertainment on a Sunday dinner, Monday night, or any other time of Sky's choosing.

Money talks and Britain's football clubs have listened carefully.

The game has been modernised, sanitised and commercialised.

Some might even say: *sterilised*.

Today's football fans can enjoy a safer environment within modern stadiums, complete with better facilities and all mod cons. But at what cost?

What has been the price that we have paid to remain a part of this re-branded, re-packaged commodity?

What else has been lost along with the terraces?

This book turns back the clock... reverses the changes of the past 30 years... and allows the reader to experience football as it was, seen through the eyes of some of those fans all that time ago... back to an age that was far more meat pie than prawn sandwiches!

1. THATCHER'S KIDS

In 1981, a punk rock band called the Angelic Upstarts released their third album; it was called *Two Million Voices*. The album title was a reflection of the unemployment figure in Britain at the time the record was made. By the time the band begun to tour the album, the true number had risen to become a lot closer to 3million.

Youth unemployment in particular had increased dramatically in the early '80's, forcing tens of thousands of kids straight from school and onto the dole. This was at a time when the traditional apprenticeships offered to school leavers were, in many cases, being replaced with the newly introduced Youth Opportunities Program. It was a time when a broken Britain offered no-future to many of its young.

Almost inevitably, 1981 witnessed large-scale riots in many inner city areas across the full length of the British Isles. The protests were mainly directed against youth unemployment, but also against policing methods and the Government's policies in general.

Thatcher's Tories had been in power since 1979 and as Britain headed towards an upcoming General Election, their days seemed numbered. The country had become very much a divided nation.

However, opportunity knocked in 1982 when Argentine forces invaded the Falkland Islands. Thatcher's 'Churchill-like' response proved popular with the electorate, as she committed a large British task force to the South Atlantic to reclaim the islands.

Her victory against the Argentine Junta of General Galtieri bolstered the Tories' standing in the opinion polls, and this proved to be the cornerstone for their landslide election victory of the following year.

Thatcher was both loved and hated as she continued to divide Britain with her policies. But she will be always be remembered by many people for the privatisation of Britain's utilities and its heavy industries.

At the start of her second administration, this course of action brought her into direct conflict with the miners and their union. Her plans for large-scale pit closures were overwhelmingly opposed by the miners, and inevitably they went out on strike in March 1984. It was a fight that Thatcher had purposely picked and was well prepared for.

On Wednesday 7th March 1984 – just one day after the proposed pit closures were announced – Nottingham Forest were due to play the Austrian side Sturm Graz in the UEFA Cup Quarter final 1st Leg at the City Ground.

I was going to the game, driving there myself and giving lifts to a couple of mates, Scrawn and Dave Illingworth.

We had met at the New Inn public house and set off for the match in plenty of time. As we all got into the car, I started the engine and switched on the tape deck, turning the volume up a notch or two.

The aforementioned Angelic Upstarts' *Two Million Voices* record blared out of the speakers as we set off to see the game.

Like my car – which was a 1978 T- registration Mini – most of the music on my tapes was old, or in the case of the Upstarts, still a few years past. The tapes reflected my love of punk rock. My record collection reinforced this to the point that I didn't have anything else but punk. Although I did own a couple of Status Quo singles that had been given to me by my mates. Even then, they never got played.

The journey was short. We all lived in Kegworth, which was bang in the middle of nowhere: ten miles from Nottingham, ten miles from Derby, and just under twenty miles from Leicester. It was Nowhere City!

Another quick beer in the Trent Bridge Inn, then off we went to see the game. Dave stumped up 40p for a programme. We entered

1. THATCHER'S KIDS

the ground to stand in the Colwick Road part of the ground. This was where we stood for most games.

In the late '70's we used to stand in the Trent End, which was Forest's home end. But since about '81 we had shifted to the Colwick Road at the opposite end of the ground – next to where the away fans stood.

The only shortcoming of this change was that it was an open end, with no roof. This meant that we were open to the elements, and so the correct choice of clothing for the game was essential. Dave Illingworth was so spectacularly bad in his selection of what to wear that the rest of us would generally wait to see what he did, then make the opposite choice. It is a wonder that Dave didn't get pneumonia more often than just the one time that he did.

The match itself was disappointing, with the Austrians defending stubbornly and Forest struggling to create many chances. Fortunately for the Reds, Paul Hart – Forest's central defender – managed to score the only goal of the game. But with the away leg still to come, Forest's expected progress in the competition was somewhat in doubt.

Back in the car after the match, the mood was subdued, with Scrawn and Dave debating the possible outcomes of the tie.

Scrawn was very much a glass-half-full type of guy, and he fully expected Forest to sail through and 'get it right' in Austria. Me and Dave were less confident. Nevertheless, as we listened to Stiff Little Fingers on the tape deck, we were hoping that Scrawn would be proved right in his assessment of the situation.

Scrawn remained confident. He usually did, never one to be found lacking in self-belief in his own abilities in general. I'd known him since we were at school and had been going to Forest with him since I was old enough to drink in the pubs around the ground. He was two or three years older than me – and in truth, me and the rest of my mates sometimes looked towards him for a bit of guidance, drawing on his extra experiences of life.

In football terms, this experience included more than the odd punch-up. And when I first started going to games with Scrawn, the gang we hung around with contained a few more like-minded individuals. These were lads who never really went looking for trouble, but never looked the other way if it found them. There were some great characters and good mates amongst them. They were a reflection of their times; fans like Botty, Todd, Kempy and 'Bloodbath Jim'.

Trouble at football in the early '80's wasn't something you could always guarantee to avoid, particularly when travelling to matches away from home. I certainly wasn't someone who looked for it, but sometimes it was almost unavoidable. When it did find me, I quickly worked out that the choice was simple: you have to try to protect yourself.

You either defend yourself or you run away.

The first time that I went to Old Trafford back in 1978, I went with a few of my mates from school. Being young, we naively thought that sticking close to the police horses at the front of our police escort would be the safest bet for getting into the ground in one piece. It seemed like a good idea in theory.

There were over 55,000 at the game that day, and it felt like most of them were lined up along the route that our police escort was taking us. As we all marched past the baying United fans, a copper picked up a pool ball off the road just in front of me – as the United fans on either side jeered and chanted at us.

As we approached the forecourt at the front of the ground, there was a large group of United fans waiting for us to arrive and it looked like it was all going to kick-off. The police quickly anticipated this potential trouble, and the mounted police at the front of our escort galloped forwards to disperse the group and avert any possible clash.

1. THATCHER'S KIDS

Doing so, they left me and my mates completely isolated. It was only now we realised that, by keeping up with the horses at the front of the escort, we had left the rest of the coppers and other Forest fans twenty yards behind us. The United fans closed in on the four of us and we were incredibly fortunate. The only thing that saved us from getting a slap was that the United fans took pity on us shit-scared kids. On this occasion that was enough to save us from a kicking, but it wasn't always the case.

But life is about learning from your mistakes and trying not to make them twice. This was a valuable lesson and one I tried to heed.

I soon realised it was safer to stay with those that were in the same boat – the other lads – because sticking together offered the best form of protection.

So by 1984 I was a little more streetwise, thanks to a combination of learning the hard way through such experiences, going to loads of games, and mixing with some older more 'worldly' lads such as Scrawn.

But being a football fan in the early '80's meant having to avoid a whole range of pitfalls when going to watch games; it wasn't just the opposing fans. At this time the police and stewards at the games were a law unto themselves, and getting arrested or being thrown out the ground was commonplace.

You didn't even have to have actually done anything; just being a football fan meant that you were already guilty. Absolutely anyone could fall foul of the law and it was so easy to get into trouble.

As my mate Tommy soon found out to his cost.

Like me, Tommy was also a punk – and in March '82 when we went to see Forest's home game against Ipswich Town, he was wearing a black punk jacket covered in badges, safety pins and zips.

He had an 'Anti-Pasti' patch that covered the whole back of his jacket.

Half-time came along and I told Tommy that I was going for a piss.

He said he'd come along, just to stretch his legs. So we went to the toilets at the back of the stand. Tommy stood outside whilst I went in for a piss.

When I came back out, no more than a minute later, Tommy was being questioned by two police officers. One of them was speaking on his radio and as I went over to see what was going on, I heard this copper giving a full description of Tommy's appearance.

Now as well as being dressed head to foot in full punk gear, Tommy's only 5 foot 2 inches tall. He was wearing National Health glasses and sporting a distinctive hair cut. To say that he stood out from the crowd would be an understatement!

The officer continued to describe Tommy's appearance over his radio, right down to the Anti-Pasti patch on the back of his jacket.

"It's him!" said the copper excitedly as he then put his radio away.

Next minute, Tommy's being asked to answer multiple questions: name, date of birth, where you been, what you done, have you got an alibi?

All the time this was happening, the other copper keeps saying to Tommy, "Go and have your piss and then we'll be off."

He repeats this at least half a dozen times, each time choosing to ignore the fact that Tommy's telling him that he doesn't need one.

Eventually the coppers take Tommy away with them, off to the police cells situated behind (what was then) the Executive Stand.

Fifteen minutes later and the arresting officers returned to their position in the Colwick Road end of the ground where I was standing. "Excuse me, what's happened to my mate?" I asked them.

They said he'd been taken down to the Meadows police station to be charged.

I left the ground straight away, and ran down to the cop-shop to find out what the bloody hell was going on. When I got there I went straight to the front desk and asked if Tommy had been brought in.

Before the desk sergeant could answer me I heard a door open loudly, and into the room walked four or five policemen. At second glance I saw that standing right in the middle of them, completely surrounded, was Tommy.

Tommy 'allegedly' fitted the description of a man wanted by the police for a stabbing that took place not far from the football ground earlier that evening.

Unfortunately for Tommy, his alibi was that at the time the incident took place, he was at home in Kegworth with his mum watching *Crossroads* on the television!

Not exactly in keeping with his punk rock image!

Hearing that, the police offered him some more time to rethink his story again, and he was on his way back to the cells just as I had walked in.

I told the policeman on the desk that I had been with Tommy earlier in the evening and so straight away I was taken for questioning.

After giving them my name and address the next question they put to me was, "Have you got form?"

"No, nobody's given one to me," I replied. I realised from the look on the copper's face that I'd said the wrong thing. The penny dropped and I realised he meant 'form' as in criminal record.

"No, I've not," I added quickly, correcting my error.

The copper wasn't sure whether I was trying to be clever or was just stupid. Unfortunately I have to confess it was the latter.

I managed to convince them that Tommy had been with me at the time of the stabbing. I had stopped for petrol before leaving Kegworth, providing Tommy and myself with an alibi that proved we couldn't possibly have been in Nottingham at the time of the stabbing.

After a short deliberation, Tommy was released without charge and we were even offered a lift back to the match in the back of a police car.

We accepted, and we were dropped off right outside the away end.

"You'll be OK going in here lads," the cops told us.

With only about two minutes of the game left, we ran up the stairs and onto the terracing in the away end. I just had time to see that the scoreboard showed that it was now 1 – 1, before a loud voice shouted,

"You two – fuck off back out or you're nicked."

We weren't going to go back down that route again!

The second leg away to Sturm Graz took place two weeks later. I listened to it nervously on the radio. Yet again it was another drab game that was nowhere near a classic. After 90 minutes the Austrians had done enough to send the tie into extra time, leading 1 – 0 on the night.

With just six minutes of extra time remaining and a penalty shootout seeming almost inevitable, Forest were awarded a penalty.

Colin Walsh converted it and I kept listening as Forest thankfully held on to win 2 – 1 on aggregate, and reach the semi-finals of the UEFA cup.

The result was greeted cheerfully by me and my mates, and Scrawn immediately came up with the idea that we should travel to see both legs of the semi-final – home and away!

I'd already been fortunate enough to see Forest play away in Europe before. I went to Cologne with my school mates, and then I travelled to Munich with my dad and my uncle for the European Cup final against Malmo in 1979.

But it had been the following season's journey to Ajax that had proven to be my real eye-opener, to say the least.

I made the trip to Amsterdam with a bus load of fans from a pub in Shepshed, called The Ox Lea. Scrawn was one of the lads with whom I went with to see the game. There were seven of us from in and around Kegworth, with nearly all of the rest from Shepshed.

Before the match the famous red light district was awash with Forest fans, and not surprisingly we were amongst them. My mate Carl and I had only just turned eighteen and I was still at school, so I didn't have that much money. We'd never seen anything like this before in our lives! Though we enjoyed the sights and the experience, neither of us had the slightest intention of actually going with a prostitute.

We were very much just window shopping!

However, it wasn't long before one of the gang of lads we were with suggested we all chip in some money and draw lots – with the winner getting the girl, so to speak. Straight away, most of our group were well up for it.

Carl and I were far less enthusiastic, but we said nothing in the face of the idea's overwhelming support.

Scrawn started to collect everyone's money and I reluctantly paid up but also added that I didn't want to be included in the draw. That was deemed fair enough with everybody else; it meant that the others now had a one in six chance of winning, not one in seven. Straight away Carl echoed my proposal, saying that he wasn't interested in being in the draw either. His offer was also accepted.

As we continued our walk through the red light district, looking for the likely lady, two of the other lads had been chatting and they announced that they too no longer wanted to be included in the draw.

This meant there were now only three left in.

At this point the three remaining candidates started moaning about the rest of us dropping out, and suggesting that everyone should be put back into the draw and take part.

I argued that if someone didn't want to go with a prostitute but still chipped in their money, where was the problem? It just increased the chances of those that actually wanted to!

The rest of the lads who shared my point of view backed me up, leaving the three remaining lads as still the only candidates in the draw.

This led to even more deliberation. In the end, two of the remaining three also dropped out. That left Scrawn as the only one not to bottle it, thus making him the 'winner' by default.

All that remained now was for him to pick his 'prize'.

But as we continued to tour the red light area in search of the lucky lady, Scrawn began to get agitated – until finally he backed down too.

"Fuck it" he said, "If I shag a prostitute, the story will be all round Kegworth before I even get back!"

I'd had a result. I even got the money back that I'd chipped in!

"You can count me in," I told Scrawn, as we continued to discuss the potential trip to the semi-final away leg.

I thought Dave Illingworth was a near certainty for it as well, having already travelled up to Glasgow to see Forest knock Celtic out of the cup in an earlier round. However, he said that possible work commitments put his chances of going in doubt.

Surprisingly the only other person who showed any real interest was Ian Webster, or Webby as he was known. Webby was, in truth, a Derby fan – but he liked to watch all the local sides play and he often came with us to watch Forest. He saw himself as an England fan first and foremost; club football was secondary.

Even the ever-positive Scrawn looked disappointed that out of all our mates, only three of us seemed serious about going.

But at this stage we still didn't even know where we might be going to.

When the draw was eventually made, it paired Forest with Anderlecht of Belgium, who played in Brussels. This was perfect. The location made travel relatively easy and would help to keep costs within reason.

The first leg of the semi-final was scheduled for the City Ground on Wednesday 11th April, with the return leg in Brussels two weeks later.

The dates unfortunately meant that Dave Illingworth was unable to get out of his work commitments for the away game. He was gutted. That meant in all likelihood it would be just Scrawn, Webby and me sailing out to support the Reds over in Belgium.

1. THATCHER'S KIDS

Away from the EUFA cup; Forest were also having a good time of things in the league. They had managed to stay in the top five for almost the whole season, and were now threatening to attain their highest finish for some time.

But there was no escaping the fact that it was Forest's run in the UEFA Cup that had captured the imagination of me and my friends.

It now seemed ages since the previous September, when we had seen Forest beat Vorwaerts in the first round – a tie in which the Reds had won both the home and away legs. They achieved the same feat in the next round, with PSV Eindhoven suffering the same fate. Then the third round saw Forest drawn against Glasgow Celtic, in what was the tie of the round.

Over 34,000 had packed into the City Ground on a freezing November evening, to see a 0 – 0 draw where the atmosphere at the game was far, far superior to the quality of the football being played. But with a tricky away leg at Celtic to come, it looked like Forest's cup run could be coming to an untimely end. Then against all the odds, Forest went to Glasgow and won 2 – 1 in front of a crowd of almost 67,000.

Sturm Graz were the next team to be beaten in the quarter-final, and now Forest faced Anderlecht with a place in the UEFA cup final on offer to the winners.

The home leg against Anderlecht couldn't happen soon enough, such was our excitement. Forest prepared for the semi-final clash with a 3 – 1 home win against West Bromwich Albion in the league, whilst we warmed up for the game with a couple of pints in the New Inn.

There were five of us going to the Anderlecht home game; Scrawn, Dave, Webby, me and Johnny Woods – who at seventeen was the youngest amongst us and still at school. Five would've been a tight squeeze in my mini, so Scrawn agreed to drive to the game in his Cortina Mk4.

Scrawn proudly called it the 'General Lee' after the car in the *Dukes of Hazard* TV show. But the only real similarity was the fact it had four wheels.

The journey to the ground was very much the norm for a drive with Scrawn: composed motoring. He was always content to take his time and let the world around him get on with its business. That is, until we reached the outskirts of town. Then for whatever reason, as soon as we entered any speed-restricted area it was game on. It became Brands Hatch – Scrawn never gave an inch and never missed an opportunity to overtake or even undertake. In those days, long before speed cameras, nothing got past him. Nothing!

Sure enough, in next to no time, we were parked up and already walking to the ground.

The crowd that night was 22,681 – which was well above the season's average. But we all thought the number disappointing, given that the game was a UEFA Cup semi-final.

The first forty-five minutes produced that same feeling of disappointment that always accompanies a goal-less first half in a need-to-win game. Forest had started well enough, but Anderlecht defended resolutely and looked to be a threat on the break. At half-time, we all said Forest needed to take a lead into the second leg, but again only Scrawn was confident of us actually being able to do so.

After the break, Forest started the second half with much greater purpose. Cloughie had seemingly given them a bollocking at half-time, to good effect. Yet still Anderlecht defended well and, despite the pressure, Forest were still unable to score. As our anxiety increased and time began to run out, Steve Hodge finally broke the deadlock to send us all blissfully mental. We were all still jumping about, going mad, when just a few minutes later he scored again. 2 – 0. Pandemonium!

The two late goals and a clean sheet was more than we could have dared to hope for. It was a great result, and it put Forest securely into the driving seat to reach the final. Bring on the second leg; all of us now shared Scrawn's confidence. We returned back to the New Inn in fine spirits, and celebrated our victory with more than a few beers.

More than ever, we were looking forward to our Belgian excursion. Anderlecht here we come!!

2. THREE BECOMES FIVE

Britain was a bleak place that spring. The miners' strike was now well underway, and job prospects amongst the nations' young were appalling.

Unemployment figures were to peak in 1984, at 3.3 million people out of work. Britain's youth was still the part of the population worst hit, and it left many of them feeling that they had no real hope and no future.

The Youth Opportunities Programme, created in 1981, had been badly designed. Its aim was to help ease school leavers into full-time employment. The trouble was that because it was deeply flawed it had failed miserably. It was replaced in 1983 by the equally abysmal Youth Training Scheme (YTS).

The YTS was widely abused by employers. It provided businesses with a source of cheap labour, whilst offering little or no training or education for those young people unfortunate enough to be put on the scheme. The government failed to act, possibly because they benefitted from the fact that those on the YTS did not appear in the unemployment figures.

Those on the scheme were earning precious little more than the dole money they would have been entitled to get, without working at all.

One of our mates who'd been forced to work on the scheme was Dave Tilling. He was just one of many. And, like a lot of others, he certainly wasn't too happy about it!

He worked on one of the local farms. Long hours and hard work for shit money. Farmers are notoriously tight and the YTS scheme gave them even more help in exploiting their young workers. Not that they needed any help or encouragement.

Till – or 'Crazy Till', as he was known for reasons that will soon become apparent – was out with us drinking in the Cap and Stocking pub a week or so before our trip to Anderlecht. After a couple of beers, he was once again rightly bemoaning the hours he was putting in at work, and the amount of money he was taking home in return.

Something didn't add up, and it was hard not to sympathise with him.

Till came from the school of hard knocks. He had always had it rough, he had learned to take what life threw at him and roll with it.

He got blamed for everything at work, blamed at home and blamed wherever he went. He felt he might as well do whatever he wanted, because he was doubtlessly going to get the blame for it anyway.

Six months earlier, Till had been on a night out in Long Eaton, along with the rest of us. We'd all caught a taxi home at the end of the night and duly arrived back to Kegworth just before midnight.

All of us were a little bit drunk, but whilst the rest of us went home, Till and another one of our mates stayed out. In a drunken stupor, they picked up a bench and proceeded to smash all of the windows in the public toilets.

The landlord of a nearby pub heard the noise they were making, and he was later able to identify Till to the police. Although Till was prosecuted, he refused to name his accomplice. He took it on the chin and ended up going to court alone.

At his trial, the pub landlord was called as the prosecution's chief witness.

"I heard a loud noise, that I believed to be the smashing of glass," he told the court.

"I looked onto the market place where I could see Tilling and another man smashing the windows in the public toilets," he continued.

"Then I heard Tilling shout: 'Yabadabadoo what a great fucker!!'"

The local newspaper loved that story!

Till was a staunch Derby fan and as the conversation changed back to football he reluctantly conceded that the best chance that he had of going to see Derby play in Europe, would be if there was another war.

2. THREE BECOMES FIVE

"So why don't you come with us then?" said Webby. "I'm a Derby fan and I'm going."

On the face of it, Webby's suggestion would seem to be a perfectly reasonable question – but not to us it didn't. Till coming with us was something we wouldn't have thought of, and hadn't even considered.

Whilst Webby was a Derby fan himself, he had often been with us to Forest in the past, so it seemed sort of natural for him to come along.

But Till went to games with the DLF (Derby Lunatic Fringe) – Derby's hardcore support. Home and away, he was Derby through and through. He was prepared to shed blood for the cause, and had done.

Surely, he wouldn't even want to come? And, if he did, we didn't know just how welcome he'd be. We'd not given it any consideration.

Till did consider it, but not for too long,

"Yeah OK, I'm up for it. Why not?" he said, to everyone's amazement except Webby's. "Sounds like a crack!"

Me and Scrawn just looked at each other, aghast. It was sheer madness.

All of us Kegworth lads were mates, regardless of which team we supported. Derby, Leicester, Forest, whoever it may be, we all got on. My brother's a Leicester fan and I've got as many mates who support Derby as Forest. But the thought of Till coming away with us to Anderlecht hadn't even entered into my head.

It just shouldn't really happen. It couldn't happen.

But it was happening. Crazy as it seemed, Crazy Till had become the fourth member of our little group who would be travelling to Anderlecht – in what was now just a few days.

We almost expected that he would change his mind once he'd sobered up. But no. He booked a week off work from the farm, and proudly announced to us that he was going to get absolutely plastered abroad!

Later that same night whilst we were drinking in the Cap and Stocking, Scrawn told us in amongst the usual banter that he was Kegworth's fastest runner, quickest driver, best bar-football player, and so the list continued.

Foolishly I rose to the bait, despite the fact that I should have known better. I threw the gauntlet down, challenging him at bar-football.

Having beaten him several times in the past I knew I could give him a good game, whilst also remembering that he had beaten me more often than not. Problem was – since the Ex-Servicemen's club had been closed down, not one of the other pubs in Kegworth had a football table.

The Ex-Servicemen's club was forced to shut its doors following a police undercover operation at a strip-show. (It all happens in Nowhere City!) So the only table we could use locally was at the Kegworth Youth Club.

Just two days before we're due to go to Anderlecht, about six of us – all aged 18 to 24 – piled into the local youth club to 'borrow' their bar-football table. This was not the first such invasion; table tennis or bar-football challenges often led to the use of the youth club's equipment.

It proved to be a close fought battle, but sadly for me it was one that I ultimately lost. Scrawn was triumphant.

He let me know in no uncertain terms who was number one!

Just as soon as we had finished playing, the door opened and in walked our friend DD.

"I thought we were all meeting in the New Inn at 7.30," he said.

"Does it look like it?" said Scrawn, in the full knowledge that it was now after 8pm and we had only just finished playing bar-football.

Webby intervened, explaining there had been a slight change of plan due to the bar-football, but we were on our way there now.

"Hey up DD, what are you doing next week?" said Till, completely out of the blue. "Why don't you come with us? We're going to see Forest play in Belgium."

"Are you going then?" said a very surprised DD. "You're going to see Forest play?"

2. THREE BECOMES FIVE

"No mate, I'm not going away to see Forest," said a smiling Till. "I'm going to Belgium for a bit of a holiday on the piss!"

DD played football for one of the Kegworth teams. But as much as he loved being on the pitch, he wasn't really into watching professional football at all.

In truth, he didn't really have a team that he followed.

So the thought of going to Belgium to watch Forest – or anyone else – play was never really going to appeal to him at all.

However, the thought of a few days away on the piss... well, that was an entirely different story.

DD quickly caught up on exactly who was going, how long for and how we were going to get there. By then we had a fifth member on board, and now with just two days to go until we were due to depart.

DD had only just turned eighteen, but was very much a part of our little gang. He'd been coming out drinking with us since he had left school a couple of years earlier.

Scrawn had taken DD under his wing a little. Like the rest of us, he was delighted that we had a further quality addition to our numbers.

Everything was now arranged. Or, to be accurate, everything was going to be arranged as and when it was required.

In fact the only firm plans we really had were to meet up in the Cap and Stocking at Saturday dinner, travel to London in Webby's car, and then stay one night in North London before sailing on to Belgium the following day.

The rest we would figure out as we went along. The game was afoot.

3. THAT'S THE WAY TO DO IT

Saturday 21st April 1984 was a lovely warm sunny day and spring was very much in the air. My excitement was practically uncontainable as I packed my travel bag with my clothes for our trip to Belgium.

Punk t-shirts accompanied Kappa and Pringle jumpers, with Fred Perry polo shirts and my Lonsdale sweatshirt thrown in for good measure.

I was a hybrid of punk and football casual clothing. The bag contained a mishmash of who I was, rather than what looked good.

I checked that I'd got my money and passport. Job done.

I reminded mum and dad that I'd be home on Thursday, and I'd see them then. And I was off.

"Hope they win... take care of yourself... and don't get into trouble." Those were the last words that I heard as I left the house and walked towards the Cap and Stocking pub, just a hundred yards or so away.

I was the last to arrive. Scrawn, Webby, Till and DD were already assembled, already drinking, and all ready to go.

The mood was one of excitement. There was a lot of banter flying about, lots of laughter, and a lot of anticipation. I got the beers in and Scrawn got up to put some more money in the jukebox.

The Cap and Stocking jukebox was from another age. None of us knew quite how old it actually was, but most of the records on it dated from the fifties and sixties. One play was an old sixpence, which was no longer legal tender and hadn't been for quite some years. However you could still get three plays for 5p – or 'a shilling' in Cap talk.

Thankfully Keith, the landlord's son and a fellow Forest fan, had persuaded his dad to put a few more modern records on the jukebox. Although I use the term 'modern' very loosely.

Scrawn was a big fan of the Boomtown Rats and it was no surprise to the rest of us that he selected both sides of their *Someone's Looking at You* single, as well as choosing the ever popular *Paddy on the Railways* by the Dubliners.

By the time the records had finished playing, DD and Till were itching for the rest of us to drink up and set off for the big city.

We chucked our bags into Webby's car boot. To say that Till and Webby were travelling light would be an understatement. Now fully loaded, we set off for London – Scrawn in the front with Webby, the rest of us in the back. Within two hundred yards, we had already stopped for lunch at Charlie's Fish and Chip shop.

It took the best part of two and an half hours to make it from Nowhere City central to North West London. A time that passed all the more sweetly thanks to the Buzzcocks and the Toy Dolls.

Unbelievably, we found the road and the house where we were staying with no problems whatsoever. Out we got and we all stretched our legs. Scrawn had arranged for us to stay at his brother in-law Howard's house. He barely knew the lad that his brother in-law had bought the house with, and the rest of us had never seen either of them prior to the trip. Bags in hand we all walked up to the front door, where there was a note that they had left for us.

'Gone to QPR see you all later' it read. Bollocks!

After a brief discussion we decided to dump our bags back in Webby's boot and then go for a walkabout, to get to know the place.

We set off in no particular direction, selecting our route by what looked to be the most promising avenue. It was now nearly 3pm, so all the pubs were already shut. We were just killing time.

It was more by luck than judgement that we managed to stumble across the local underground station.

"Come on, let's go into the city. See what's happening in town!" was DD's call to arms. But Till had a better idea, or at least in his own mind he did.

"No, let's all go to see the Arsenal versus Spurs match," he said excitedly with a great big smile right across the full width of his face.

But neither idea proved popular with the rest of us, Till's plan being dismissed mostly because the game would have already kicked off before we got there.

In truth, we doubted that watching the match was the real reason Till wanted to go. This theory quickly proved to be correct when he decided that he was still going to go anyway.

He said he would meet us back here at the tube station at six o'clock after the game. Then off he toddled, all alone, down to the platform and merrily on his way to the North London derby.

The rest of us spent the afternoon just mooching around. We went into a few shops, but generally we just killed time whilst waiting for our hosts to return from Loftus Road.

We got back to their house shortly after 5pm. They joined us soon after, and we now met Howard and Steve for the first time.

Howard and Steve owned the house jointly, and they had a lodger living with them as well. Originally they had both lived in Loughborough, which is just seven miles from Kegworth, and they had stayed down in London after going to university there. They were very welcoming and both of them seemed genuinely nice lads.

Scrawn and DD stayed to chat with them, whilst me and Webby headed back to the underground station to meet Till as we had arranged.

Crazy Till was once again smiling from ear to ear when he met us, only fractionally later than the arranged time. He was full of what had happened after the Arsenal versus Spurs game, detailing events that had taken place and the various people that he'd met. He carried on for a good ten minutes, never once bothering to mention the score or even who had won the game. He was buzzing!

Whilst we were still in the vicinity, Webby wanted to have another look in one of the shops that we had visited earlier that afternoon. We went in and, although I could see nothing of interest, Webby and Till seemed keen on some of the gear. Eventually Webby decided against buying anything, but Till got himself a new t-shirt. It was a beige Pierre Cardin t-shirt with a "v" neck. Till thought it was the dog's bollocks.

We then took a slow walk back, returning to the house to find the other lads almost ready to go out.

"Come on, get a move on," said Scrawn. "We're all going to go to Covent Garden."

Now we didn't get to go out in London very often, so that gave us plenty of motivation to get ready in double quick time and then set off to catch the tube into town.

The two lads we were staying with led the way. As we walked to the tube station I sensed that something seemed a little bit different, and it wasn't just Till's new t-shirt.

I wasn't quite sure what it was, but something was amiss.

Soon the train arrived and we all got on. It was busy, the carriages already full of likeminded people setting out for a Saturday night on the town.

In the same carriage as us, there were a large group of people wearing fancy-dress. Most of them were dressed as cowboys, which seemed to cause great hilarity for Scrawn, DD, Webby and Till.

Then I finally clicked on to what I had sensed earlier: they were all high!

The four of them had dropped acid – which was not that unusual – but I had not realised they'd already done it that night.

The train came to a halt at a station along the route. A few people got off and a few more got on. But the train remained stationary. It didn't move for some considerable time. Passengers quickly become impatient, wondering what was going on.

3. THAT'S THE WAY TO DO IT

After a while, there was an announcement that there would be a delay, due to a fault with the train. Another one would arrive shortly.

So we all got off the train and stood around on the platform, waiting.

People began to sit down and settle into the fact that we may be stuck here for some time. Till was the first of our group to sit himself down on the platform. As he chatted to the rest of us, he unwittingly wiped his hand across his face, which left a black mark.

It was nothing more than a transfer of dirt off the platform onto his hands and then onto his face.

The black mark on Till's face resulted in Scrawn breaking into a fit of laughter. The other lads also noticed it and, albeit to a lesser extent, Webby and DD were also laughing. But Scrawn was crying out loud.

It wasn't even all that funny, but poor Till had no idea what they were all laughing at and was completely baffled.

The more he tried to find out what was the cause of their laughter, the more they laughed at him. As Till grew increasingly agitated by the laughter, he kept rubbing his head, transferring more and more black grime. In no time at all, he was looking just like one of the Black and White Minstrels!

Even I was laughing now. But Webby and DD were completely pissing themselves, and by now Scrawn was laughing so much that he almost fell onto the train rails.

The other passengers began to give us a wide berth. It was crazy. We were literally falling about with laughter, for no other reason than Till had a few black marks on his face.

None of the other passengers understood what was going on. It was very much a private joke. We weren't so much on another wavelength; we were on another planet!

Only the arrival of the relief train stopped our antics from descending fully into madness.

We arrived to find that Covent Garden was heaving.

Making our way through the crowds of revellers, we only walked a short distance before we found our way into the Punch and Judy pub. We got the beers in and wandered around the pub, chatting and joking as we went. For a while we stayed pretty much together, then we began to split up and mingle with other people in the bar.

I got talking to a couple of Chelsea fans who were stood at the bar. They seemed to be solid lads, very friendly and good company. After talking to them for half hour or so I made my way back to the others.

The pub was packed and locating them proved to be more difficult than I had expected. Eventually I spotted Till and Webby, who were sat at a table all on their own.

"Where are the others?" I asked them, but I got no reply.

I repeated the question but Till just grinned inanely at me. Webby just looked like he'd fallen asleep with his eyes open.

"Where the fuck are the others?" I asked for a third time, now with more than a touch of frustration thrown in for good measure.

Till was now laughing his little head off but still apparently unable to speak, whilst Webby was, in my own estimation, completely off his face!

I gave up on them and headed back to the bar.

The Chelsea lads had gone, but fortunately for me there was still plenty of beer left in the pub. I ordered a pint; the signs were that I was going to need it badly. I took my beer and headed back to the two clowns I'd just left upstairs. A glutton for punishment, I tried again:

"Where have the others all gone?"

And as if by magic, Till – still grinning stupidly – just about managed to explain to me that they had left for another pub, but they would be returning here later.

So it's Saturday night. I'm in a packed pub in the middle of Convent Garden, suitably attired, but I'm stuck with Dumb and Dumber!

3. THAT'S THE WAY TO DO IT

I drank my pint and fetched another and still Webby says nothing.

Then Till suddenly stands up and without saying a single word, he takes his permanently grinning mush and heads off into the crowds.

Not a word; he just gets up and walks away!

I'm now thinking that this can't get any worse.

I made one last desperate attempt to start a conversation with Webby. Eventually seeing the error of my ways, I gave it up as a bad job.

So I got up and went to look for someone else to talk to.

Nobody in particular.

Just someone who could actually speak would be an improvement.

I looked around, and despite the pub being really busy I soon noticed a young woman standing alone. She was looking out over the pub balcony, scanning the room.

"Are you waiting for someone?" I asked her, asking the blatantly obvious.

She said she was waiting for her friend to join her.

I quickly learned that she came to London most weekends, catching the train in from Hertfordshire. She seemed to be friendly enough and we carried on chatting, just passing the time together.

Suddenly we were interrupted.

"Ayup my duck, how are you then?"

It was Webby – seemingly back from the dead and right on cue, with an absolute vengeance!

He followed up his question by just staring intently at the poor girl's tits, whilst waiting for her to reply.

The now terrified girl seemed instantly transformed into a petrified rabbit – transfixed in the headlights of an oncoming juggernaut!

She appeared to be totally paralysed, whilst I was totally amazed that Webby had actually somehow managed to regain his power of speech.

Webby just continued to stare at her tits.

Time stands still. The three of us just standing there. All of us lost for words.

"Who's this then?"

And just when you think it can't get any worse: Crazy Till makes his return to the real world and wants to know who it is that Webby and me are talking to.

Fortunately for the young lady in question, her mate arrives and they both leave as fast as their little legs can carry them.

"Come on," says Till, "we're going to another pub."

The other lads had now returned back to the Punch and Judy. They had sent Till up to find me and Webby, to tell us that we were all moving on.

4. THE BIG CITY

The fresh air hit me for six as soon as we had left the pub. I'd felt reasonably OK prior to leaving. But when we got outside, I immediately knew that I'd had a drink. Again it was only a short walk before we arrived at our next port of call.

Outside of the pub there was a chap busking, playing his accordion.

Before we entered there was a bit of commotion, with Scrawn insisting on having a go on the bloke's accordion. The busker was having none of it, but eventually he and Scrawn reached a type of compromise. Scrawn accompanied him as he played, by indiscriminately pressing various keys on the accordion – much to the busker's annoyance.

The pub we'd arrived at was very traditional, a stark contrast to the one we had just left. The atmosphere was more relaxed and once again the clientele were very friendly. We quickly settled in and had a couple of drinks.

In what seemed like no time at all, the lads we were staying with said we needed to drink up and leave, in order to catch the last tube back home. We did so and headed off towards the tube station, with them leading the way again. When we reached the tube station's side entrance, we found that it was already shut, meaning that we now had to race around to the main entrance. Too late – that too was now shut. Bollocks!

Now the only option available was to get taxis.

There were seven of us, so we needed to find two. We didn't have to wait for too long before the first one arrived. It made perfect sense for Steve and Howard to go in the first taxi, so they could open their house up for the rest of us. Scrawn and DD jumped in with them, and off they all went.

It was a case of déjà vu. It definitely felt like we'd been here before. I looked around and I could see no one else but Webby and Crazy Till.

I feared the worst!

A few minutes passed. Then another taxi arrived and we all jumped in.

"Evening lads, where are you going?" asked the cabbie.

His simple question was met by a wall of silence. Shit!

Not one of us could even remember the street-name of the house where we were staying. We all suggested several ideas and possibilities, but the names we mentioned didn't sound right and none of them meant anything at all to the driver.

We knew roughly where we were heading to. The best I could offer was NW10. Collectively we managed to throw in both Harlesden and then Willesden as possible destinations, but in truth we were completely clueless.

Finally I remembered that we'd all walked down to Willesden Junction earlier in the afternoon, and thought we should just about be able to get our bearings from there.

Despite our inability to even give the taxi driver an address for where we wanted to go, Crazy Till still felt confident enough to tell the driver not to rip us off by taking anything other than the shortest route home.

"This isn't the right way," Till insisted at least four times, as we motored through the night and across the city.

The monotony was only interrupted when Till suddenly and excitedly shouted for us to look out the taxi windows.

"Look, look, it's the Libyan embassy!" he insisted.

And as we looked out into the blur of the night, amid the concrete and the dark shadows, there was in fact a road that had been cordoned off by the police. We could just about make out various vehicles and a number of people, in position further down the street.

4. THE BIG CITY

Just four day earlier, there had been an anti-Gadaffi protest outside the Libyan embassy. During this protest against the Libyan dictator, a young British policewoman named Yvonne Fletcher had been shot dead. Witnesses and reports claimed that the shot was fired from inside the Libyan embassy and this situation had quickly escalated, with the police eventually laying siege to the embassy.

"That was definitely the Libyan embassy", Till once again insisted. "Definitely," he reassured himself over and over.

The rest of our journey was relatively uneventful, with only the odd "This isn't the right way" interrupting the silence.

The taxi stopped once we had reached Willesden Junction. We paid the fare, got out and watched the cab speed off into the night.

I looked around. It now seemed nothing like the place where we had walked to meet Till earlier that evening.

By now it was gone midnight and, whether due to the darkness or the drink, I was struggling to get my bearings.

I hoped that one of the others might come to the fore and rescue the situation. Then reality hit and I remembered who I was with.

"Have you got any ideas then lads?" I asked, confessing my inability to remember the right way.

Again it went deathly silent, so I took that to be a 'no'.

Each of the possible directions looked as unfamiliar as the next, with nothing coming to mind that gave any indication of the route to take.

Eventually, we chose a direction, for no reason other reason than it looked to be the busiest road. There weren't many people about, and asking for direction would be virtually impossible given that we couldn't even remember the name of the street we were looking for. We carried on walking.

After a while we came across a takeaway which was still open.

We went in and got some chips. We went through the pointless exercise of asking directions to a road for which we couldn't remember the name. Not surprisingly, it proved fruitless.

We walked as we ate our takeaway, yet still we saw nothing that was familiar to us. I thought we should turn around, as we couldn't recognise anything that we might have seen earlier. Webby suggested that we walk a little further in the current direction.

We were at a dead loss.

As we stood, deliberating upon the best course of action, voices in the distance broke the silence. We looked down the nearest side street, and saw there was a large group of blokes stood about laughing and joking in the road. My instincts told me that we should make a move and carry on with our search, hiding that we were completely lost as best we could. But before I had a chance to put my proposal into words, Till already had another idea.

"I'll go and ask them if they know the way," he told us.

"Don't go down there mate," I urged him. But it was too late. Till was already on his way.

I had a feeling things were about to go from bad to worse. It intensified as the blokes surrounded him while he walked the fifty-odd yards to where they were standing.

From what we could see, there seemed to be a quick conversation, then a few raised voices and then two of the blokes got in to a car. Till followed suit, getting into the same car. It drove towards us, stopping right in front of us.

The car window wound down,

"Jump in!" shouts Till. "I've got us a lift!"

To be honest, I still wasn't sure what the hell was happening, but Webby got straight in the car and so I followed him. Only once that we'd got in did I see exactly who was in the car. There were two black blokes in the front of car, with Webby, Till and me all in the back. The two guys in front looked

4. THE BIG CITY

to be in their mid- to late-twenties or possibly early thirties. Both of them were big blokes.

Being local, they had somehow managed to figure out the street we were looking for from the vague details Till had given them, and had then offered to give us a lift home. It all seemed too good to be true. We thanked them for picking us up and things seemed fine and as we drove. I even began to notice one or two familiar places from earlier in the day. We seemed to be on the right track.

Till then struck up a bizarre conversation with them – asking if they knew some black lads that he was mates with back in Derby. Unsurprisingly, given they lived 120 miles away, they both confessed to not knowing any of the lads that Till mentioned.

Then suddenly, the car screeched to an absolute halt. It was like something straight out of *The Sweeney*! My heart was in my mouth, and I was wondering what the fuck was happening. I was just about to shout to the others for us to leg it, when the driver coolly winds his window down and starts chatting to one of his mates, who he'd just spotted walking down the street. Panic over!

The guys all have a bit of a chat, and in next to no time we set off again. A few seconds later we're back at the house.

The blokes in the car had been absolutely brilliant.

Not only had they been able to put us back on track, but they had also given us a lift home as well. They'd never seen us before, they've never seen us since, they were only in our lives for ten minutes or so. But they put themselves out for us.

They were proper gentlemen.

When we walked into the house, DD and Scrawn started to laugh their heads off at us. Neither of them had given us any chance of being able to find our way back. I doubt they ever realised just how close to being right they really were.

Even though it was now the early morning, there was a full-blown house party still going off right across the road. They had speakers in the garden, people everywhere and the volume of the reggae music was full on. Welcome to the big city!

Till suggested that we should have a wander over and invite ourselves in.

The rest of us managed to talk him out of it, our hosts in particular explaining that it wouldn't be a particularly good idea.

But with the music as loud as it was, there was no point in us trying to get any sleep. So we all ended up watching video recordings of *The Young Ones*. I think all of us had seen the episodes before and funny as they were, they soon became the background to the various conversations we started up.

After all the beer that had been drunk earlier, we were all still laughing and joking and generally in high spirits. However the mood suddenly changed when Scrawn asked Howard where their lodger was, noting that he hadn't yet returned to the house.

Very quickly it became apparent to us that the lodger was not popular.

Our hosts told us that he hadn't paid any rent for some time and he had become increasingly obnoxious about it, basically telling them to fuck off whenever they broached the subject.

As is so often the case... just as we all sat around discussing him, in he walked. The room fell silent.

"I take it you're all talking about me?" he guessed correctly. "Well whether I pay my rent or not, it's got fuck all to do with any of you lot!"

He paused briefly, then continued his rant.

He went on to tell us that he had just 'kicked the shit' out of two blokes up the road, and held out his bloodied hand for us to see the proof of his conquest.

4. THE BIG CITY

Very quickly he singled out Scrawn as being the most likely of us to stand up to him, so he quickly rounded on him.

"How about you then eh?" he said, offering it to Scrawn. "Do you want some eh, do you want a go?"

Surprisingly to me, Scrawn sat there and just let it go.

Not a peep back in response.

After this, the room fell silent again, with only the music from across the road to be heard. A few minutes later, Scrawn got up and solemnly walked out the room.

That was that, I thought, and I felt that now would probably be a good time to think about getting my head down for the night. The rest of the lads all remained quiet, so the only noise inside the house was coming from the lodger, who was once again giving it the big 'I am'.

We did our best to ignore him, in the hope that he'd eventually shut up and go to sleep. Then the door opened and Scrawn re-entered the room. He was now bare-chested, stripped down to just a pair of trainers and his jogging trousers.

"Me and you best go outside and have a little talk," said Scrawn, and the lodger duly obliged him.

They both stepped out the room and the door shut behind them.

"Oi!" I said to the others. "Get ready. If it kicks off, we're all in."

Enough was enough and everybody nodded, they knew the crack.

We listened to the conversation going on outside our room, as Scrawn and the lodger argued then talked. It got quieter and quieter.

After ten minutes or so, we were all half watching *The Young Ones* again, when the door re-opened and Scrawn walked back in and told us:

"You had best call an ambulance. This guy's going to need one."

As he walked back out of the room, he picked up a big glass ashtray. Seconds later, the thumping barrage of noise from the house party across the road was obliterated by the screams that came from the room next door.

I jumped straight up and ran towards the room where Scrawn and the lodger were. With the rest of the lads behind me, I burst in to find Scrawn seemingly in mid-air, punching, kicking and battering the shit out of the lodger, who lay in a ball on the floor.

Scrawn then proceeded to reshape the radiator with the lodger's head. We literally had to pull him off the lodger. I got splattered with blood as we strived to save the lodger from getting absolutely murdered.

Scrawn then told Howard to pack some of the lodger's clothes into a bag. He threw it down the stairs, telling the lodger to fuck off in no uncertain terms.

With the excitement over, we all sat down again to watch the remainder of the *Young Ones* video. Scrawn had a shower, got dressed and then rejoined us.

Till was still trying in vain to persuade us to venture across the road to the house party, even though it was now 2am.

As he looked out the window to see what he was missing across the road, Till spotted that the lodger was now over there. He was seemingly trying to gain some sympathy from the partygoers.

The blasting reggae music meant that we had no idea what he was telling them, but the fact that he was pointing over at our house gave us a pretty good idea.

Given the time, with the speakers in the garden across the road still at full blast, it was no real surprise that the police would turn up there at some point during the evening. That time was now.

They quickly succeeded in getting the music turned off, ending the night's proceedings. Peace at last.

This was the cue for all of us to settle down for the night. I was tired and could feel sleep creeping up on me very quickly.

4. THE BIG CITY

At first I thought that I must be dreaming. But the knocking at the door wasn't imaginary, and it wasn't going to go away. Someone went down and opened the door, and in walked the lodger again.

This time he was with the police.

One of the coppers explained to us that an allegation of assault had been made, and then asked the lodger to point out his alleged attacker.

He looked around the room, his stare fixing on each of us in turn then moving on to the next person. He looked at Scrawn twice, before telling the coppers that the person responsible must have already left. Fortunately for us, he was suffering so badly from concussion that he was completely unable to identify Scrawn.

The police then asked who owned the house, giving Howard and Steve a chance to explain to them the problems they'd been having with their lodger. They mentioned the threats he'd made over the non-payment of rent, and they made it clear to the police that they wanted him out of the house. This position was then clarified to the lodger by the police.

Our hosts had got a result. Their lodger had at last received his comeuppance, having been advised to leave the house by the police.

Add to that, we'd all had a top night out in Covent Garden – so all in all it had been a busy, but successful day.

But now we were knackered and it was time to get some well-deserved rest. Tomorrow we were crossing the waters, and Europe was beckoning. Here we go!

Through the Seasons Before Us - Following Nottingham Forest in the 80s

5. ALL ABOARD

I awoke Sunday morning feeling quite all right, surprising given the excesses of the night before. As I looked around the room I could only see Webby who was also already awake.

As the two of us began to recall the events of the previous evening, I found myself continually shaking my head in sheer disbelief at our antics.

Our chatting woke the others and soon everyone joined in, recounting their own versions of the previous night's escapades.

Our timing was spot on. We had given ourselves enough time to avoid having to rush for the train, and we weren't up far too early.

It meant that we were able to get ready for the forthcoming journey at our leisure.

But it didn't take us long to wash, dress and be ready to leave.

We each thanked Steve and Howard for their hospitality. Then we headed off to catch the tube to London Victoria station, where we were boarding the boat train to Dover.

Webby and I got a couple of the Sunday newspapers for us all to read on the train. I started off as usual, firstly reading the match report of Forest's game the previous afternoon. I already knew the score; they had beaten Birmingham 5 – 1. But I enjoyed reading the additional detail. The papers got passed around between us and before we knew it, we had reached Victoria station.

We still had almost an hour to wait before our train was due to leave for Dover, giving us plenty of time to get ourselves some breakfast.

Next job after that was to get some beer for us to drink on the train journey.

Even with us being in the centre of London, this was no easy task on a Sunday morning back in 1984. We searched without any success for an off-license which was open, and eventually we split up to increase our chances of finding somewhere.

DD and I searched around but drew a blank. We were on the verge of giving in when DD spotted a pub. We tried the door but to no avail. Hardly surprising, since it was still well before opening time. Nevertheless we tried again, and then strained our eyes in an attempt to stare through the stained glass windows.

"What's up lads?" said a voice unexpectedly,

"We're just trying to get a beer mate, that's all," we explained.

"Try the door round the side there lads," came the helpful reply.

"Cheers".

Seconds later we were in the pub and walking up to the bar.

The open side-door was undoubtedly an arrangement for the locals. As we walked in, the landlord looked at us very warily before finally serving us with the drinks we had ordered.

Time was running out fast, meaning that we had to drink up quickly if we were to get back to the station in time. But before leaving the pub, we completed our original objective by getting a take-out for us all to drink on the train. We met up with the others, boarded the train and settled down in a compartment that we had claimed for ourselves.

"Do you like that shirt Till?" DD enquired, drawing everyone's attention to the fact that Till was wearing his new Pierre Cardin t-shirt for the second successive day.

The joking and piss-taking continued, as the train pulled out of the station and began the short journey down to the coast.

Before too long, DD, Till and me all decided that we'd have a scout around. Take a walk up and down the train, just being nosey, seeing who was on, as you do. We stopped for a brief chat with some young Americans who were on our train. When we returned to our carriage, we found Webby now sitting all alone.

5. ALL ABOARD

"Where's Scrawn gone?" asked DD.

"He said he was going to the bog" said Webby, almost dismissively.

Nothing more was thought of it until fifteen minutes or so later, when Scrawn still hadn't returned. We became intrigued, and wondered exactly what he was up to. Out of curiosity we had a quick look up and down the train, to see if there was any sign of him.

We couldn't see him, but I did notice that one of the toilets nearest to our carriage was locked. Eventually I thought that I'd just check it out.

"Scrawn, is that you in there mate?" I said, knocking on the door.

"Yeah, what's up?" was the puzzled reply.

"I'm just checking mate".

Five minutes later and Scrawn finally returned to our compartment with his wash-bag under his arm. Somehow, he had managed to shampoo his hair and have a shave in the train toilet as we headed down to Dover.

Scrawn put his wash-bag away, back inside his travel bag, and told us he would see us later. With a twinkle in his eye, he headed back down the train.

It hadn't taken long for us to drink the beer that DD and I had got from the pub earlier. With that now gone, Till decided that the day still needed livening up a bit more, and he dropped an acid tab there and then.

He tried desperately to get DD to do the same, but in this instance DD resisted the temptation.

"Come on," I said, "Let's go and see what Scrawn's getting up to."

We wandered through the carriages until we finally spotted Scrawn.

He was sat opposite a very attractive woman, who looked to be in her early twenties. What we couldn't see at first, and only realised once we got closer to where they were sitting, was that the woman also had a young child with her, who was no more than a toddler.

Thankfully we managed to adopt a far more reserved approach than had been our original intention. We just stopped briefly to say hello, rather than unreservedly taking the piss.

However, much to our amusement we had still managed to catch the woman asking Scrawn how long he had actually been a helicopter pilot!

We gave Scrawn a little bit of space and left him to work his magic.

A helicopter pilot indeed!

Till was now getting more and more excitable, and told us that he was contemplating doing a rendition of the 'dance of the flaming arseholes' when we eventually arrived in Ostend.

It was just one of the many party tricks that he was happy to perform on almost any occasion.

This feat of ingenuity required the 'dancer' to stuff a rolled-up newspaper up his rectum, light the paper and then quickly drink a pint of beer before removing the newspaper – fast enough that you don't burn your arse!

I'd seen Till perform this stunt on a fair few occasions, but by far the most memorable was his performance at the Fosters pub in Kegworth a couple of years earlier.

We had all had a fair few drinks, the night was going well and we were cajoling Till into performing. He didn't need a lot of persuasion and he quickly agreed – but only if someone bought him the pint of beer to do it with.

So up Till gets, he's now standing on a stool in the middle of the pub. Trousers down around his ankles, waiting for his pint and a newspaper.

I brought his beer over, but nobody could find a newspaper anywhere. Shit!

Someone then came up with an idea to save the day: get some toilet paper, and use that as a substitute for the newspaper. We were back on.

5. ALL ABOARD

Till placed what he thought was a decent length of toilet paper firmly up his bum, and then prepared to drink his pint as fast as he could.

"Ready, go!" someone shouted.

Woooooff!

As soon as the toilet paper was lit, it burned so fast that the flames reached Till's arse within a split second. By the time he had put his drink to his lips, his arse was already burning. Till realised this... briefly thought about it... but stubbornly started to drink his beer.

"Aaargghh!!" Till shrieked in pain – and he reluctantly pulled the paper out of his arse with almost a full pint of beer still left to drink.

It was an all time classic!!

For poor Till, there was still worse to come. The next day his burns were so bad that he had to go and see the doctor. Till was once again asked to drop his pants so that the doctor could examine his burns.

"And how exactly did your injuries occur?" asked the doctor.

Till said that the doctor couldn't stop himself from laughing when he explained exactly how they'd been caused!

As Till was reminded of this occasion, he recalled that he had not been able to sit down for over a week. Every time he tried, the blisters on his arse kept bursting, making it look like he'd pissed himself.

The recollection of this tale was enough to put him off any repeat performance in Ostend, and he soon withdrew his offer.

"Here we are," exclaimed Webby, and I looked up to see the 'Dover' sign out of the train window. We'd arrived.

As we did so, Scrawn returned to our compartment to get his bag.

"Here's Biggles," said DD. Scrawn wasn't going live down his 'I'm a helicopter pilot' line very quickly.

We all got our bags and made our way off the train.

The port was close by, and we sauntered slowly down the platform towards the port buildings. Scrawn was walking alongside his new friends and was still embellishing the truth, shall we say.

From what he told her, he had apparently been in David Bowie's latest video; if you look very carefully, he's stood just behind the star. We made sure we stayed close enough to hear their conversation.

The funniest part of it was that she was swallowing it – hook, line and sinker.

As we entered the buildings, we found ourselves waiting in a long queue to get through Customs. Rather than standing in line, we all sat down and waited for it to clear. Scrawn eventually rejoined us, and he too seemed in no particular hurry to get through Customs.

We waited until the queue had virtually disappeared and then we all got up to join onto the end of it. As I started to walk towards the line, Scrawn shouted me back.

"I can't go," he said, but offered no real reason.

I was totally shocked and wondered if maybe he had a fear of sailing.

"You'll be alright mate. We'll be in Ostend before you know it."

"No, I can't go Kingy," he said. "Look at my passport!"

I realised what the problem was. His passport had expired. It was well over a year out of date!

The other lads were already going through Customs, looking back at us and wondering what the hold-up was about.

They looked astonished when I walked through customs on my own – leaving Scrawn behind, unable to sail with us.

I was faced with a barrage of questions on getting through Customs and catching up with the others. I told them that Scrawn's passport was over a year out of date. But whilst that provided an answer as to why he couldn't sail with us, it wasn't really any kind of explanation.

It had been Scrawn's idea to make the trip in the first place. He'd had weeks to go and get a new passport. None of it seemed to make any sense whatsoever.

5. ALL ABOARD

We were all downcast. Scrawn wasn't just our friend. More than anyone else he was usually the one who got us all doing things, as well as sorting stuff out. It still didn't really sink in.

Through the Seasons Before Us - Following Nottingham Forest in the 80s

6. WE'RE ENGLISH, WE'RE BARMY!

It certainly didn't sink in with Crazy Till – because despite managing to keep his shit together whilst going through customs, he was now bang up for it once we had got on the boat.

The 'boat' was in fact a Jetfoil, a type of hovercraft that ran between Dover and Ostend. It had cost us a little bit more money, but it cut the crossing time to just over an hour and a half.

Being onboard felt a little bit like being on a plane, in as much as you were sat in rows and had to remain seated at given times.

Shrewdly, we strategically sat Till down between DD and me. He was already attracting a bit of attention and was once again chomping at the bit for yet more beer. We thought we had better try to calm him down, try to keep him under control. There was no chance.

Just like on an aircraft, there were 'attendants' serving food and drink to the passengers during the channel crossing. And just the same as on a plane, this was done in systematic order.

Order or not, it didn't stop Till calling out for a beer long before the stewardess was due to serve us. And no matter how many times we told him to wait, it made no difference.

Eventually Till's belligerence paid off, and one of the attendants served him with the beer that he had been shouting for. For a little while, he was apparently content and he happily drank his beer.

Not long afterwards, the rest of us also got served drinks.

Till shook his can, and determined that it was almost empty. So he purchased another, and decided to get a ham salad roll to go with it. At least whilst he ate his roll it kept him quiet – although, in all truth, he spread as much of it over his face as he managed to eat. It was not a pleasant sight.

The temporary quiet was rudely interrupted when Till had spotted that the stewardesses had finished serving, and it looked like that they were taking the drinks trolley away.

"Whoa!" shouted Till. "I'll have another beer please!" This was said with a large portion of his ham salad roll still in his mouth.

He waved his arms about for good measure, determined not to miss the opportunity of one last drink.

The stewardess couldn't help but notice him and came over. But there was no way she could possibly have interpreted his initial order.

"Can I help you sir?" she enquired, with far more courtesy than he deserved.

"Yeah, I want another beer," Till spurted – completely showering her with bits of half-chewed bread and salad.

Her immaculate appearance was now pebble-dashed with bits of Till's afternoon snack. It wasn't a good look.

To her credit she still served Till with his beer, managing what must have been a forced half-smile as she did so.

"Cheers," said Till, once again happy now that he had a drink in his hand.

"What?" he asked, glaring at DD and me as we both shook our heads in amazement at his shocking behaviour.

Not only had the crossing been shortened when we opted to go via Jetfoil, it was also a lot more comfortable. A much smoother ride. Hovering above the waves negated the swell of the sea, reducing the motion that can often cause sea-sickness. Unfortunately for us, we had only booked it the one way; we were coming back on the ferry straight after the game – late Wednesday night, early Thursday morning.

Webby had been very quiet for most of the crossing. But as land came in to sight, he quickly perked up. Soon we could see the harbour and then we were in it, docking not long after that.

6. WE'RE ENGLISH, WE'RE BARMY!

Only as we gathered our bags to disembark did it once again dawn on us that we would be setting out without Scrawn. Still... as big a loss as that was, we weren't going to let it stop us from having some fun.

We left the Jetfoil behind us as we slowly made our way into the Customs area. Talking as we walked, none us had noticed the large chalkboard that had been placed strategically at the side of the walkway. Written on it was important information for a specific passenger who had been on our crossing. Remarkably, it was for me!

'Would Mr King please meet Mr Tarlton off the next Jetfoil?'

There it stood, written in large letters on this chalkboard in Ostend: confirmation that Scrawn would be rejoining us on the next Jetfoil.

We were amazed that we should be greeted in a foreign country by a message written just for us. Even more puzzling, though, was how Scrawn had managed to be able to come – given that we knew his passport was out of date. For the time being, that didn't matter. What did matter was to find out what time the next Jetfoil was due to arrive.

We asked a couple of likely people that were working in the port area, and they both told us the same time. 6.30pm.

That gave us a couple of hours. Just long enough for us to go and find somewhere to stay before coming back to meet Scrawn.

Or at least that was the plan that most of us had in mind.

Whilst we were piecing together the details for us to meet up with Scrawn, Till had got chatting to some English lads who'd crossed on the same Jetfoil. They were going on to Italy from Ostend and – with a couple of hours to kill before their train was due to leave – they had decided to go on the piss for a while. Till quickly decided that he was going to join them, so we left him to it.

By now we were inside Ostend train station, which merged into the port. Till agreed to meet us back here at 6.15pm, when we'd all then go and meet Scrawn.

We walked into Ostend, looking for suitable accommodation as we went. Anything cheap and cheerful would suffice. There were plenty of choices, but none that stood out from the rest. We had far from exhausted our options when Webby spotted one called 'The St George'.

"That's just got to be the one!" said Webby.

It was too much of an omen to turn down, and so Webby led DD and me into the hotel to enquire about a possible vacant room.

Our luck seemed to be holding when we approached the reception desk to be greeted not only in English, but also with an English accent.

So we were terribly disappointed when the landlady sadly informed us that we were out of luck, and all the rooms were already taken.

But she was quickly interrupted by her husband, who reminded her that the family room on the top floor was now free.

"Will it sleep five?" DD asked, and an affirmative answer left us with our digs now sorted. DD and I handed over our passports as collateral, and we paid a deposit for the room. We followed the landlord up the stairs to the fourth and top floor of the hotel.

It was a small family-run concern, with just six or seven guest rooms. The stairs were steep and narrow and they snaked round and round as we climbed them to the top.

Our room was big enough; it had a double bed and three singles. There was no bathroom as such, just a sink and a mirror.

"The toilets are at the bottom of the stairs on your right," said the landlord, leaving the best bit of news until last.

I chucked my bag on the bed furthest away from the sink. I could already sense what was going to happen. Webby and DD followed suit, selecting the beds that they wanted for the next couple of nights.

No messing about. We dumped our bags and came straight back down, ready to leave, with the plan being to reunite us all – first meeting Till, then Scrawn.

6. WE'RE ENGLISH, WE'RE BARMY!

Then we would all be set for a night on the town in Ostend.

It sounded simple. How could it possibly go wrong?

Ostend train station was a busy junction, with passengers using it to continue their journeys from the port to destinations all over Europe.

At 6.15pm that evening it was no different, and trying to spot Crazy Till amongst the masses of travellers wasn't helped by the fact that he was not at the agreed meeting place.

We gave him the benefit of the doubt and waited for him. But after a further 10 minutes we faced the dilemma of deciding whether to hang around for Till, or go to meet Scrawn – who would be getting off the Jetfoil at 6.30pm.

Meeting Scrawn came out as a priority, so we set off to catch up with him again.

To ensure he had a proper welcome, we managed to smuggle ourselves into the area of the port where his craft was actually docking. This way, we would take him completely by surprise. We managed to achieve this with relative ease, feeling pleased with ourselves for our ingenuity.

His Jetfoil had already arrived, so we waited as the rest of the passengers disembarked. We looked for Scrawn amongst them, a task that became more and more manageable as the stream of passengers tailed to a trickle.

Everyone was now off the boat and there had been no sign of Scrawn. It was certainly possible that we could have missed him, but it was also feasible that he hadn't even been on-board. We just didn't know. It was as simple as that.

It now also dawned on us, that without our passports, we couldn't just follow the rest of the passengers off the ferries and through Customs. So we had to sneak out the port the same way that we had got in, which thankfully proved ridiculously easy once again.

Before trying to track down Scrawn, we first had to find the elusive Till. We went back into the train station where he still hadn't shown up at the agreed meeting place. We decided a quick search of the train station would be in order, to eliminate any misunderstanding regarding the exact spot where we were due to meet.

There followed a fruitless search by DD, Webby and myself, splitting up and scrutinising the crowds of people as best we could. No joy.

Just as we had decided to break off the search, DD spotted something odd about one of the many annexes that surrounded the station – providing seating for travellers whilst they waited for their trains.

All of the other annexes were full, with all the seats taken. Yet although the one DD had pointed out was still busy, it had a notable gap where no one appeared to be sitting.

With nothing to lose we went over to have a closer look and, bingo!

Sprawled out across several seats was a very-much-the-worse-for-wear Crazy Till.

"Till!" Several times I spoke, getting louder each time, accompanied by an increasingly vigorous shaking of his shoulder. It was pointless.

"Oi Till!" This time I slapped his face, gently but repeatedly, waiting for some kind of recognition or reaction. Still there was nothing.

Now all three of us were trying to cajole some sign of life from him. Physically slapping, shaking and pulling him about to trigger a response. Eventually, in a scene that resembled the rebirth of Frankenstein's monster, Till very slowly stumbled back to life.

He struggled pitifully to his feet, his balance seemingly having deserted him. He was toppling and staggering from side to side, with only the walls of the annexe preventing him from falling over.

Crashing from one annexe wall to another, he created an ever-growing space around him, as the other passengers gave him a wide berth.

Still rocking from side to side and taking two steps forward and three steps back, he raised his arms above his head and slurring all his words, he chanted:

6. WE'RE ENGLISH, WE'RE BARMY!

"We're English, we're barmy, we're out our fucking heads!"

"We're English, we're barmy, we're out our fucking heads!"

I'll say this much about Till – he didn't always get everything right, but he was spot on with that song!

The next task we faced would be a difficult one: trying to get Till booked into the hotel without getting the rest of us thrown out in the process.

Again we had a plan. I'd take Till's passport and deposit, and book him in as quickly as possible. DD would take his bag up to our room. Leaving Webby to mind Till, hopefully keeping him in order.

The walk back to the hotel from the train station had seen a slight improvement in Till's condition. He was still none too stable on his feet, but the power of speech had certainly returned to him – which meant we didn't go too long before we would be treated to another rendition of 'We're English, we're barmy, we're out our fucking heads!'

"Just stand there Till, say nothing and don't fall over," just about summed up the only advice we could think to give him as we entered the St George Hotel once again.

DD went upstairs with Till's bag whilst I went to the reception counter and booked him in. I handed the landlady his passport and deposit, just as we had planned.

Now it had not gone unnoticed by Webby that the landlady was rather buxom. As he cast his admiring glances in her general direction, it was all Till required to slip away and strike up a conversation with the landlord.

"You're all big Forest fans are you then?" I heard the landlord say.

"No, not me mate," said Till, "I've only come for the trouble!"

Whether the landlord thought he must be joking, didn't hear him or didn't really care, he let it go.

DD returned downstairs, and so we set out for the night with the intention of trying to locate Scrawn – not knowing for a fact that he had even arrived in Ostend. The only evidence to say he was actually coming was the message scribbled on a chalkboard.

Again we split into two groups to cover as many different bars as possible, as we searched Ostend as best we could. Every 30 minutes or so our two groups would meet up, then we would do it all over again, searching a different area each time.

After an hour and a half we'd covered countless bars but to no avail.

We took a short break from our search to go for a beer together and have a rethink.

We had only been drinking for five minutes, when in walked a lad that I used to work with. He was called Dick Durant.

I was amazed to see him so far from home, but he seemed none too surprised to see me.

"I've just been talking to your mate," he said, confirming once and for all that Scrawn had actually arrived in Ostend.

Dick had travelled with his local football team, and after having played a tournament in Belgium they were now relaxing before sailing back to England later that night. It was good to see him and catch up and he gave us directions to where he'd met Scrawn earlier.

We reached the bar where Dick had bumped into Scrawn, but he was no longer there. We split into two once again: DD and Till; Webby and me.

Though we searched, there was still no sign of Scrawn, so we returned after 30 minutes just as before. But this time there was no Till or DD either.

"They must have found him," concluded Webby, more in hope than expectation.

With this in mind, we traced the most likely route taken by Till and DD and went searching for them. Within a couple of minutes we'd managed to locate DD.

6. WE'RE ENGLISH, WE'RE BARMY!

"Where's Till?" asked Webby.

"I've bloody lost him!" said a frustrated DD.

Things were not getting any better.

DD told us that he and Till had been together right up to a couple of minutes earlier, so we knew that he wasn't too far away.

"He's here look!" Webby spotted him almost immediately. There he was, sat in a café all on his own.

DD marched straight into the café – at exactly the same moment Till's food was arriving at his table.

DD paused. Then he went over to the counter, where the waitress gave him something that we couldn't quite see.

Till looked shocked when he saw DD approaching his table. He soon looked a hell of a lot more shocked, when DD picked up his plate and tipped its contents into the paper bag he had just got from the waitress.

DD marched out of the café carrying Tills food, followed by a soulful Till chasing after him in protest.

"The sooner we find Scrawn, the sooner we can all get some food and have a few beers," said DD, with the emphasis on 'all'.

"I didn't realise they did takeaways Till?" Webby taunted.

This time we stuck together as we continued our search.

Bar after bar after bar, but still we had no joy.

Then, just as we least expected it… there was Scrawn, walking down the same street but in the opposite direction, heading straight towards us.

I think he must have spotted us at exactly the same moment as we spotted him. Our quest was over. We were finally once again united.

7. ALL ABROAD

Scrawn explained to us that he had only managed to get permission to travel by doing so on a 72 hour pass. That meant he would have to return to Britain by Wednesday tea-time – which would be before the game was even due to kick-off, later that evening.

The news was far from ideal. But at least Scrawn was here now, which was a lot better than him not being able to travel at all.

It was something to celebrate, so we headed for the nearest bar and we all raised our glasses. Several times.

With Scrawn still not booked into the St George hotel, we headed back there about 11pm. We found a mix of guests and non-guests having a night out, using the hotel bar and all its facilities.

The St George bar had its own pool table, and that seemed to be the centre of the action when we returned.

After booking Scrawn into the Hotel and showing him up to our room, I went back downstairs to find that DD had already got the beers in.

"Webby's up next" DD said, meaning on the pool table.

"I'm surprised he's still standing!" I replied, in reference to the amount of beer that Webby had drunk over the course of the day.

The pool table in the hotel was typical of the ones we'd seen in a lot of the bars around Ostend. It had large pockets, and in the St George the balls were larger too. At the table it was 'winner stays on' – and there was this one bloke who looked a bit hot, seemingly beating everyone.

It was now Webby's turn to play him. Webby was a decent player, but in truth none of us expected him to win. The odds were stacked against him. Different size balls to those in England, bigger pockets, he didn't yet know the speed of the table and – most importantly – the fact that he'd been drinking all day! Not to mention that he was up against a good, albeit cocky opponent.

As we predicted, the game was over quickly. But it was Webby who had won, leaving Mr Cocky with four or five balls still on the table.

The bloke wasn't too happy, particularly as he must have been able to tell that Webby had been drinking. He put some more money down for a return match.

Much to our delight, Webby managed to keep up his form, beating a couple more challengers before Mr Cocky was back on.

"Come on Webby!" We were all right behind him... cheering him on, applauding every shot he made. Webby didn't disappoint and won again.

This time Mr Cocky didn't even bother with another challenge. He'd had enough and left the hotel bar – cue under his arm, tail between his legs!

"Enger-land Enger-land Enger-land!" We gave it to him as he walked out.

Scrawn was the next opponent up for Webby. As with most things, Scrawn fancied himself as a pool player. He broke, and a ball went in.

"You're stripes," said Webby.

"10 ball in the centre pocket," said a confident Scrawn.

"12 ball in the corner right," Scrawn continued and again potted it.

"13 in the centre," he nominated, but this time he failed to deliver.

"Unlucky for some!" Webby replied.

Webby came back into the game and fought his way to a tight finish. Scrawn only had one ball left and Webby the same, but it was Webby's turn at the table.

"You're going to miss this," Scrawn said, looking for a psychological advantage. It worked and Webby missed. But fortunately the balls ran kindly for him, and left Scrawn snookered.

"Jammy bastard," Scrawn bemoaned, but Webby just smiled.

7. ALL ABROAD

Scrawn missed and left Webby with two shots, a position from which he cleared the table.

"Jammy bastard," Scrawn repeated and chucked more money down.

But before any rematch could take place, Webby had to beat DD and me first. He did it in some style, seeming to get better and better.

"These balls are like footballs Kingy, I can't miss," he said, almost apologising for thrashing me.

Scrawn now returned to the table and announced that it was revenge time. Not yet it wasn't. Webby won far more comfortably than before, and he remained undefeated. Me and DD both tried again but went the same way, beaten easily and leaving Webby with no challengers left to play.

It had been a long day, and I for one, was ready for some sleep. Scrawn and DD said they felt the same way, but Webby told us that he was going to stay downstairs and play a little longer. He set the balls up once more. This time he was sure to win again; he was playing by himself.

Whilst the rest of us had been playing pool, Till was stood at the bar talking to some guy who was in the army. Till himself had recently joined the Territorials, and with that in common the two of them were soon chatting away like the best of friends.

"We're going to bed Till," DD told him as he, Scrawn and I were walking out the bar and up to our room.

"I'll see you later then DD, we're going out for a couple of beers," said a smiling Till.

I awoke in the middle of the night and badly needed a piss. Although our room was dark, it was just light enough for me to navigate through the various beds to the sink at the far end.

Making my way back, I noticed that Webby was now back in the room having come up to bed at some point.

I had just got my head down again and was drifting off back to sleep, when suddenly I heard a loud noise.

Bang! Bang! Bang! Bang! Bang! Bang! One after another.

"What the fuck?" I thought to myself, as I sat up in bed and tried to wake myself up. My brain tried to tell me it was someone coming up the stairs.

Bang! Bang! BANG! As the noise reached the top of the stairs, DD too was now awake. He was sitting up nervously in his bed.

The door was flung open and a second or two later someone – or something – entered the room.

"Achtung, Achtung! The Leicestershire and Derbyshire Royal Yeomanry, stand by your beds!"

And with that carefully planned introduction, Crazy Till, was standing to attention in the doorway, albeit wobbling more than slightly.

His wobble proved to be temporary. It was quickly followed by him completely collapsing face first on to his bed.

This sent DD and me into fits of laughter – when, out of the blue, Webby suddenly shot bolt upright in his bed and said:

"Oh no, mam!"

And with that, he lay straight back down. Amazingly he was still sound asleep.

Before either DD or I could comprehend what had just happened with Webby, Till jumped up from his bed and dashed towards the sink – puking and retching as he went.

It was a race that Till just couldn't win.

The unmistakeable sound of someone violently throwing up continued for ages, as Till spewed time and time again.

Eventually DD and I even managed to stop laughing at him. We began to feel almost sympathetic towards Till's sorry plight. Almost, but not quite.

After all, given that he'd been drinking non-stop for 15 hours, the outcome was nearly inevitable.

7. ALL ABROAD

None of us wanted Monday morning to come as fast as it actually did. So we all did our very best to delay its onset by sleeping in as late as we possibly could. For some people, it will be remembered as the start of the day on which the singer Marvin Gaye, who made famous the song *I heard it through the grapevine*, was shot to death by his father at the age of 45. But for us, that day that be forever remembered for the terrible stench of piss and puke that drifted out from the sink in our room. It was putrid.

We slept as long as we could, trying to ignore the smell. But in the end there was only going to be one winner. Even the constant ringing of the bells from the church right next to our hotel couldn't wake us up. Those bells just didn't have the same impact as the rancid, festering odour from that toxic mix of piss and sick.

The first sign that the new day was dawning was the resumption of our joking and banter. Everyone was now awake and joining in with the piss-taking. Everyone that was, apart from Till.

He was keeping his head well and truly down.

Scrawn was the first one of us who was brave enough to leave the sanctuary of his bed. Probably because he needed a piss the most.

"Fucking hell, it's overflowing!" he said – looking disgustedly at the state of the sink, but still pissing in it anyway. "It's fucking blocked up."

Till had totally blocked the sink with the deluge of vomit he had thrown up the night before. Everyone had since had a piss, and it had just built up to leave the sink brimming with a cocktail of piss and puke.

But still nobody mentioned the terrible smell that filled the room.

As Scrawn turned around to make his return journey back to bed, he stepped bare-footed right through the trail of vomit that Till had thrown up on his way to the sink the night before.

"Fuck me, it's all over the bastard carpet!" he said in utter disgust. "Who's done all this?" Scrawn had slept through all the commotion that Till's return had caused.

Me and DD just laughed.

"Do you really have to ask?" I added.

"Till!" Scrawn had rightly determined, in answer to possibly the easiest question anyone has ever been asked.

"Oi, Till…..Till!" Scrawn was now right on his case.

Till wisely responded, "What's up?"

"What's fucking up? You've spewed everywhere, fucking everywhere!" Scrawn said, frustrated that he wasn't even able to use the sink to wash the spew from off his foot.

"You can clean it all up. It's your mess, you can clean it." He paused. "And open the window. It fucking stinks!"

Finally, we had an acceptance. Till got the message, loud and clear.

As Till started trying to clean the carpet, the rest of us got up and went downstairs out his way. We all got dressed without even being able to have a wash. With no sink, that wasn't an option.

We ordered some breakfast. And although we all smelt a little fusty, at least the room downstairs was a little fresher than the one we'd left Till to clean.

Soon the smell of an English breakfast filled the air and things were seemingly picking up. As we tucked into our breakfast, Scrawn had a moment of inspiration. He came up with the idea that we could go to the local swimming baths, where we could use their showers. We all agreed it was a great idea, and after eating breakfast we went back upstairs to get ready for a swim.

On returning to our room we found Till still hard at work.

The carpet was now reasonably clean, in truth better than we would have imagined. But the cleaning of the sink was proving to be a far more difficult task.

Despite his repeated efforts, Till was unable to completely unblock the sink and had only managed to reduce its 'sick-level' to half full.

7. ALL ABROAD

He had already resorted to picking lumps of sick out of the plug hole with his bare hands, in an unsuccessful attempt to unblock it.

"You're not leaving it like that. It's your mess Till, and you clean it!" Scrawn insisted, as we all watched Till struggle on.

To his credit, Till stuck manfully to his task. He was right up to his elbows in piss and puke, but still unable to make any real progress. Frustrated at his inability to unblock the sink, Scrawn finally decided to take matters into his own hands.

"Come out the way," he said and he moved forward purposefully, armed with a length of tubing that he had somehow acquired.

As Till gratefully stepped aside, Scrawn proceeded to vigorously thrust the tubing up and down – stabbing time and again at the area around the plug hole, attempting to free the lumps of sick that were blocking it.

This went on for some time. Although the level dropped very slightly, it didn't resolve the situation.

After a while Scrawn tired, leaving Till to take up the challenge. But again he did so with no significant result.

"Give it here," said Scrawn. "Only one thing for it." He took the tubing back from Till and wiped it dry on a cloth.

Scrawn placed one end of the tubing into his mouth and put the other end firmly into the sink.

"Fucking hell, he's going to siphon it!" shouted DD, in excited disbelief.

We all crowded round the sink, none of us was going to miss this.

Scrawn seemed all set to go, when he suddenly stopped and removed the tubing from both his mouth and the sink.

We thought he'd caught us out with the most brilliant wind-up yet. Then, just as we believed that he'd only been joking, to our amazement he again placed one end of the tube into his mouth and the other end deep into the sink. This time, it was for definitely for real.

Whooosshh!!

Whether Scrawn actually siphoned it or just blew down the tube as hard as he could, the end result was that the puke and piss exploded out of the sink, back-splashing all over the wall behind the sink.

There was only one word to describe it – un-fucking-believable!

This really was above and beyond the call of duty. Whether it was bravery, determination or just plain stupidity, Scrawn had managed to unblock the sink and save us from the rancid stench that had infested the room, whilst providing us with quality entertainment in the process.

Top marks!

We were now ready to go to the swimming baths. We had got directions from the landlord and so we set off. We took a slight detour on the way, taking in a quick walk down to the sea-front. This had been scheduled in primarily because someone had told us the previous night that Ostend had a nudist beach.

Maybe because it was still April and the hot summer weather wasn't yet upon us, there wasn't a lot of activity on the beach. For certain, there was not the procession of beauties that we had conjured up in our minds on the way down to the seafront. Needless to say, we didn't stay there very long.

Perhaps it was because we had walked past a number of bars that were already open as we went through town, or maybe they had never intended to go. But on the way to the swimming pool both Till and Webby had 'changed their minds' about going for a swim. They elected to meet us later, in the bar they were now heading to.

The remaining three of us carried on to the pool, and found it to be a superb leisure facility. It boasted an Olympic-size swimming pool, complete with diving boards, a Jacuzzi and a sauna. It was top quality.

Once we'd had a quick swim, we spent the majority of our time in the pool watching a young lady who was on the diving board. Dive after dive we watched, each time with disbelief.

7. ALL ABROAD

She was a good diver, but not great. Our disbelief came from the fact that her bikini was far too small for her ample curves, and each time she hit the water she almost lost it altogether. But every time, somehow, she managed to retain her modesty – albeit only just.

In the end it became just too frustrating. So after another quick swim, we all headed for the sauna. We spent a fair bit of time in the sauna. We were now beginning to feel human again, clean and refreshed. We were all praising the merits of going for a sauna, when I told Scrawn and DD there was one at the gym I went to back in Kegworth.

"You want to go to the one at Bramcote Swimming Baths," said Scrawn. "Go down there and you can get extras!"

"Do what?" DD asked, not believing his own ears.

"Oh yeah," said Scrawn. "They do massages and all sorts."

Me and DD looked at one another. We weren't sure where this was going.

"They'll do anything you want," Scrawn continued. "Anything! If you ask for Scotch Liz, then she'll let you have a reversible!"

"What's a reversible?" I asked, not having a clue,

"A reversible," Scrawn replied. "That's where you can massage them instead of them doing you!"

The conversation continued along the lines of whether such services would be as available in Belgium as they were in Bramcote, and just what type of girl Scotch Liz really was!

We showered and left the swimming pool, feeling all the better for the experience. It had been money well spent. We now headed off to meet back up with Webby and Till, in the knowledge that in all likelihood we'd be having a few beers.

On our way back through the centre of Ostend to meet Till and Webby, we went past a bar that seemed to be half full of English football fans.

Thinking that they might be Forest, we went for a quick look. But on closer inspection we saw that they were Man United fans, who were playing away in Italy. There were about fifteen or twenty of them, and so the three of us swerved the pub and carried on to the bar where we had arranged to meet up with Till and Webby.

We returned to find them talking to a few English lads, at least one of whom I immediately recognised.

Scrawn also recognised the same lad, both of us knowing him from Forest matches. We sat down with them and joined in with the chat.

The three lads in the bar with Till and Webby were part of a larger group of twenty or so, who'd just arrived in Ostend. They told us they were looking to join up with another group of their mates, who'd already caught the ferry over the previous day.

More Forest fans were entering the pub every few minutes, and very soon most of their mates had arrived. There were now twenty-odd of us, all having a few beers and a bit of a laugh. Some of those who had arrived on the earlier ferry said they'd had some trouble with a large group of Man United fans who were travelling at the same time. A few of them had been beaten up and had their hand luggage stolen. The rest of the lads all chipped in and made sure they were OK, buying drinks and stuff for those with no money.

There were some easily recognisable faces amongst us now, and both Scrawn and I realised that some of the lads were part of Forest's firm.

"What's the plan then? Are we going to stay out and have a few beers?" Scrawn asked the question. We all agreed that we should. It was a good atmosphere and we were enjoying the crack.

"Right then, I'm going to take my swimming kit back to the hotel and then I'll meet you back here," Scrawn decided.

"I'll come with you and dump mine," DD said, and the two of them got up to leave the pub.

7. ALL ABROAD

"Do us a favour mate," I asked DD. "Take my kit back as well. Thanks."

With DD and Scrawn heading back to the hotel, Webby got another round of drinks in for me, him and Till. By this point, one of the Forest lads had told the barman that in England beer was sometimes called 'spunk'. So all the lads were walking up to the bar and asking for three spunks or whatever.

Eventually the barman began to get the hang of it, and started to anticipate our orders. "Spunk?" he asked,

"Yeah, three spunks cheers," said Webby, holding three fingers aloft.

All this messing about added to the laughter, and the beer was flowing nicely. We settled down inside the bar – having a drink, singing a few songs and generally enjoying ourselves.

After all, this is what it was all about. This is what we had come away for.

8. FOREST BOYS WE ARE HERE!

Scrawn and DD faced a bit of a trek to get back to the hotel with all the swimming gear. They quickly began to question their decision to walk back to the hotel with their swimming kits and miss valuable drinking time. Although they walked briskly, they still had a good distance to go. Fortunately for them, salvation was close at hand.

"Here you are DD!" Scrawn half-whispered. He changed his direction, making his way to the side of the road where a pushbike had been parked. It had been secured, but not to a level that was ever going to deter Scrawn from nicking it.

"Get on quick DD," Scrawn insisted, and DD did as he was instructed – climbing on to the handlebars as the two of them attempted a quick getaway.

Their efforts were incredibly poor, and they only managed to wobble for a few yards before coming to a stuttering halt. They tried again, and once more they failed in a similar manner.

Their antics had not gone unnoticed. They had been spotted by a couple of bouncers at a nearby bar. But the doormen had no desire to intervene – they were too busy pissing themselves at the spectacle, laughing their heads off at the incompetent English bicycle thieves.

With all chance of a quick getaway long gone, Scrawn and DD eventually got their acts together and just about managed to master riding the bike in a straight line whilst still retaining their balance.

On their ride back to the hotel they became more and more adept, and their confidence grew as they improved. By the time they reached the St George, they had managed to build up a fair bit of speed and were beginning to look the part. The landlord was stood outside the hotel having a smoke when they finally reached the St George. He looked absolutely amazed to see them arrive, two upon a bicycle. He looked even more amazed as they failed to stop and flew straight past him, with DD now repeatedly shouting "Brake!" at the top of his voice.

"Where's the brakes?" screamed Scrawn. He was beginning to panic as the bike seemed to be picking up speed at a time they desperately needed to stop.

Whether it was through inspiration, good luck or divine intervention, Scrawn eventually started to pedal backwards and figured out that this was the correct way to stop the bike.

"My whole life has just flashed before me!" DD joked, as they slowed down then turned around to return to the hotel and drop off the swimming kits.

Once that was done, they again boarded their bike and set off back into town to rejoin us. Now they felt more accomplished and confident, they maintained a steady speed and made the return journey in half the time.

On their way back, DD spotted two girls who were sat out on their hotel balcony, high above them as they peddled past.

"Hiya girls!" he shouted – and having got the ladies' attention, he and Scrawn were provided with the perfect opportunity to show off. So they performed an impromptu *Butch Cassidy and the Sundance Kid*-style version of *Raindrops Keep Falling on my Head*.

Next stop was set to be the bar that they had left us drinking in an hour or so before. By now Webby and I were stood outside the bar in the sun, along with a few more of the Forest lads we were drinking with.

As we all supped our beer, a pushbike came flying in to view, seemingly from out of nowhere, with DD and Scrawn two-up on it.

Scrawn hadn't seen us and took a wrong turn, going further away from the bar where we all were all standing. At the last moment he suddenly realised where he should be heading, and corrected himself accordingly.

8. FOREST BOYS WE ARE HERE!

Quickly changing direction, he swerved right out into the middle of the road and straight into an oncoming Mercedes!

Crash!

The pair hit the car whilst still travelling at a good speed, and the impact catapulted DD off the bike and right over the front of the bonnet in true *Starsky and Hutch* style. He flew through the air, rolled across the Mercedes and landed spread-eagled in the gutter!

Fortunately he was still in one piece.

He picked himself up and dusted himself down. To his credit, he was laughing along with all of us that had just witnessed his spectacular fall from grace.

Scrawn had managed to avoid a similar fate. But he did suffer the indignity of ripping his trousers, all the way from the crutch down to the knee. The bike itself had suffered a few dents and was now slightly buckled, but it just about remained in working order.

Scrawn parked it outside the pub and they joined the rest of us, receiving a round of applause and cheers for their acrobatics!

"Five more spunks!" said Till, and so the party continued with DD and Scrawn now back on board.

After a while, everyone was getting itchy feet and we decided it was time for a change of scenery. So we made our way through the streets of Ostend, searching for another bar.

It was a sunny evening. We found a suitable place that had plenty of tables outside, situated in a small square bang in the centre of town.

The lads that arrived first walked inside and went up to the bar to get served.

"Please take a seat and we'll come and take your orders," they were told.

So we all found seats, sitting down at the outside tables. One of the lads counted everybody. When the waiter came to take the order, he was asked for twenty six beers!

Sure enough, a few minutes later and he came back outside with another waiter, both of them holding a couple of trays with all our beer on them.

Everybody helped themselves to a drink and the trays of beer were soon emptied. We were all sat outside drinking, enjoying the sun and the crack, when the waiter returned soon after and handed over a bar tab to the lad who'd ordered the beer. From the total cost, he worked out what we all owed.

Most of us paid in full for what we had ordered. But some of the lads clearly paid only a fraction of the cost or nothing at all, because our collection fell well short of the total amount.

So, knowing there was no chance of ordering another round of drinks here, after drinking up we again moved bars.

This time we didn't have far to walk, as we all headed into a lively little bar just around the corner. The staff inside were very friendly and made us feel very welcome. We stayed in there and had a couple more drinks, before once again deciding to continue our trek around the town.

"Thank you boys," said the landlord as we walked out of his bar. "If you want to come back later, we are open until late."

Leaving, we had not walked far at all before one of the lads spotted a disco. Now it was still only about 9pm, but there were a fair few of the lads who wanted to go in and have a look about.

The lads headed off inside the disco and we all followed. Not surprisingly given the time of day, there were only about a dozen people in there. So when thirty of us walked in, the bouncers took one look at us all and quickly started to panic.

It was clear that they weren't happy with the situation. But they knew and we knew that there wasn't a lot they could do about it. So, in we all went.

Not surprisingly, the few people already inside the disco seemed even less pleased to see us. That is, apart from a small group of girls who told us

8. FOREST BOYS WE ARE HERE!

they were from Leeds. They certainly seemed to enjoy the extra attention they were receiving.

Reluctantly the bar staff began to serve us all, so we each got our drinks and took our seats.

"Where's Till gone?" asked Webby, a question none of us could answer until DD spotted him. He was sitting over at the table with the girls from Leeds.

Till wasn't normally quite this smooth with the ladies. He usually took a back-seat, making way for the well-oiled machine that was Scrawn and DD.

Once when we had been to Nottingham to see Stiff Little Fingers, DD had set his sights on a couple of girls after the gig had finished, and Till was keen to help him out.

DD went in and broke the ice, chatting to the girls. Till stood with him, but allowed the master to get on with his work.

However, it wasn't all going DD's way. Despite managing to keep the girls chatting and getting them laughing, he wasn't able to seal the deal.

After DD had chipped away for 20 minutes or so, Till felt it was time to move things along. He thought long and hard, and chose his words carefully to best ensure success in their attempt to get off with the girls.

"Have you got the time?" he asked.

DD shook his head and walked away. Twenty minutes of his life that he would never get back, flushed down the drain.

All the time that we were inside the disco, there was an uncomfortable feeling. There was an edge about the place, we weren't wanted in there. For that reason as much as anything else, we weren't leaving.

The tension was mounting all time, and inevitably the mutual bad feelings resulted in to an argument breaking out. As tempers flared and push came to shove, there was a bit of a scuffle – which seemingly ended just as quickly as it had started.

"What was all that about?" I asked, unable to see from where I sat.
"Something's kicked off!" DD said, unable to add any more detail.
"Think it was a scuffle, but it's all over now!" Webby confirmed to us.

Sure enough, whatever had happened, it was now all over. It seemed to have cleared the air a little, and the arguing had stopped. The bouncers, bar staff and disco management all seemed to give us a bit more space.

Ten minutes later, and we understood why: the police arrived.

Now we're not just talking about a couple of friendly gendarmes turning up. The disco was being raided by at least a dozen police, some with dogs and most in their riot gear. Nor were they messing about. They immediately started trying to round us all up and kick us out.

Till was still talking to the girls from Leeds in the other room. It looked like he wasn't budging, and was going to stay in the disco with them.

We left him to it, and straight away DD, Scrawn, Webby and me, were all surrounded by the police. A few Forest fans had already been escorted out the disco, with the rest of us still being 'persuaded' to leave.

Those of us still remaining were objecting to being pushed about by the police. But at the slightest hint of resistance, the coppers drew their batons and released their dogs.

"Aargh!" screamed DD, with a cop dog temporarily hanging from his arm, as the cops continued to usher us out to the door. They pushed us towards the exit, herding us reluctantly outside. Just short of reaching the door, I heard another 'yelp', but this time the boot was firmly on the other foot.

Before I'd worked out where the noise had come from, a police dog came past me – flying through the air. Bridget, one of the lads we were with, had kicked the dog so hard that he had sent it airborne!

Passing through the doorway, getting outside, we were confronted by yet more police. They had formed a line across the top of the road, and we're trying to make sure that we all went in the other direction.

8. FOREST BOYS WE ARE HERE!

As we massed outside the door, some of the lads were trying to get through the cordon, only to be pushed back by the police. This was repeated again and again, usually accompanied by a bit of a scuffle as the police tried to assert their authority and restore order.

We were all outside now. The police seemed unsure whether to contain us, disperse us or arrest us. Any way it turned out, I felt it was time to make a move, and said as much to DD and Webby. As yet another scuffle kicked off outside the disco, we decided to clear off before we got nicked. So – along with Bridget and a lad called Ginger Gary – Webby, DD and me all slipped away to get something to eat.

We'd somehow managed to lose Scrawn in the fracas outside the disco. We were unsure whether he'd also slipped away or not.

"Who fancies a chinky?" DD asked, having spotted one across the road.

Gary, DD and me all ordered some food, whilst Bridget and Webby sat down without ordering anything.

When our food came it looked very appetising, but I was so hungry I could have ate a scabby donkey. As we tucked in, Webby got up from our table and wandered over to the other side of the restaurant, where some guy was sat down on his own.

The bloke had apparently finished his dinner, but he had left some ribs on the side of his plate.

"Are you finished with them mate?" Webby asked, pointing to the ribs.

The bloke gestured for Webby to help himself. He pushed his plate across the table to where Webby was now sitting.

"Cheers, you're the top man!" said Webby in gratitude for his second-hand dinner. The bloke nodded and got up to walk off into the night, leaving Webby to finish his ribs for him.

Shortly after he'd left, two Chinese guys came running out of the kitchen – armed with cleavers. They looked like they meant business.

For some reason, I thought that they were going to go for Webby. But they ran straight out the door, after the bloke who had just left without paying for his ribs!

"Fucking hell. I wouldn't like to be in his shoes if that pair get hold of him!" I said, stating the obvious.

We all carried on eating, sharing our food with Bridget as we did so.

When the door opened again, we saw that the two Chinese guys had returned – accompanied by the police.

I thought the cops must have seen them running down the street waving their cleavers about, and had nicked them. But that wasn't the case. They weren't even here for the Chinese. They had come for us!

"English?" they asked us, already knowing the answer.

"Yeah," we all replied, wondering what exactly was going on.

I started to pay more attention to the coppers, now that I knew it was us that they wanted. Worryingly I noticed that all four of them were armed.

"You," they said, indicating to Bridget. "Come with us."

One of the coppers pulled out his pistol and three of them escorted Bridget into one of the restaurant's back rooms. The fourth officer stood by the door.

When Bridget returned with the officers, he sat back down with us. Then the coppers pointed for me to go with them into the back room.

I was told to face the wall. I was spread-eagled and then searched, thoroughly.

"Name?" they asked, and followed it up by asking for my passport.

"It's back at the hotel," I answered

"What hotel?"

"I'm staying at the St George."

"Where have you been earlier tonight?"

"All over, many bars," I said, thinking I'd better be careful with my answers.

8. FOREST BOYS WE ARE HERE!

"Which bars have you been to?" they asked.

"I'm not sure of their names. Whichever ones we came to!" I replied, which on reflection wasn't far from the truth. We'd been in a fair few.

The coppers all looked at the officer asking the questions. He nodded. I was escorted back to the others and sat back down.

Ginger Gary, DD and Webby all went through a similar experience. All returned to sit with the rest of us, the cops drawing a blank.

I think all of us were relieved when shortly afterwards the coppers left. We breathed a sigh of relief. But we were also puzzled as to what it was all about.

"Jesus, they had guns!" DD exclaimed.

"What's that all about?" Webby asked and without knowing, we concluded that something serious must have kicked off earlier.

"We best go and find Till and Scrawn," I said. "See what's been going on."

We reasoned that the bar we went to earlier, where we had been invited back, would be the best place to find not only Scrawn but all the other Forest lads as well…

As we walked through town, everywhere seemed to be peaceful enough. We arrived back at the bar and, sure enough, a lot of the lads were already in there. Maybe half of those who'd been with us in the disco earlier.

Scrawn was amongst them, but there was no sign of Till at all.

"I thought Till was with you lot!" Scrawn stated. He'd not seen him since we left the disco.

"Maybe he got off with one of those Leeds girls?" I said, before remembering that for the third consecutive day, Till had once again come out wearing his Pierre Cardin t-shirt.

"Or maybe not," I added, philosophically.

The bar stayed open until late and we enjoyed what was left of the night, not leaving until it was drunk o'clock.

Whilst we were catching up with Scrawn, we told him all about our Chinese experience. Then we explained that when we were all outside the disco earlier, we had looked for him but been unable to find him.

"No wonder you couldn't find me. I didn't even know where I was!" he joked, confessing that the events outside the disco were all a bit of a blur.

Scrawn also told us that the reason the police had been called to the disco was that there had been a stabbing. Or at least, that was what everyone was saying had happened.

He said there was some more trouble with the police on leaving the disco, when some of the lads started climbing up the flag poles in the square we had been in earlier. A couple of them had been arrested for it.

After that, most of the lads had headed back to the bar where we had just found him.

When we left the bar, Ginger Gary and Bridget tagged along with us and all six of us returned back to our hotel in the early hours.

The hotel entrance was still open, but there seemed to be nobody downstairs in reception. We stayed extra quiet, given that we were smuggling two of the lads back into our room.

We made it up the stairs and into the room, undetected. Or so we thought.

But when Scrawn went back downstairs for a piss, he returned with the landlord accompanying him.

"No, there's still only the five of us," Scrawn insisted as he and the landlord reached the top of the stairs.

The landlord was less convinced than Scrawn. As he came into the room, he switched the light on and started to count us all out for himself.

"Look. There's one, two, three, four and me, five," Scrawn intervened. Demonstrating to him, counting us all out to reinforce his point.

The landlord scratched his head. He had been certain that something wasn't quite right. He counted us once again – ending up even more

8. FOREST BOYS WE ARE HERE!

puzzled when he reached the same answer that Scrawn had just given him.

He was right on the verge of leaving, when he finally noticed Ginger Gary curled up in a blanket – almost hidden from view, immediately behind the door.

"Well, who's this then?" he asked, pleased with himself for eventually catching us out.

"That's Till," said Scrawn, quick as a flash. "You've got his passport, so you know that he's staying here!"

With that, the landlord left. Not because we had managed to baffle him, more because he'd realised that whatever he said or proved, he just wasn't going to win. He was just using good old-fashioned common sense. And with that, we all decided to get our heads down.

Another day had drawn to a close, and by the time our heads hit the pillows it was now well into Tuesday morning.

Monday had brought about a crazy mixture of Olympic swimming pools, a sink full of piss and puke, a flying dog, a pushbike crash, armed police. It had ended with six of us in our room, albeit with Crazy Till still missing.

It was now too late to do anything about that, but I still wondered what Till was up to and where he was likely to be. I hoped for his sake that he'd got lucky with one of the girls he was chatting to earlier. Otherwise I feared the worse.

Given the kind of day we'd just had, I was beginning to wonder if it would actually be wiser to stay in bed in the morning. It would probably be a safer bet than catching the train to Brussels.

Still, the second leg was getting closer all the time and was now only a couple of days away. I closed my eyes and fell asleep – thinking that tomorrow would be another adventure, most probably another crazy day away on tour with the Reds!

9. THE GREAT TRAIN ROBBERY

Back in Britain, the miners were still on strike. But a division amongst the National Union of Mineworkers (NUM) was developing, and causing serious problems.

When the strike began, it did so with the miners responding to the proposed closures within their own areas. The miners in the coal fields that were affected then held local ballots to vote for strike action.

Arthur Scargill, the NUM President, then declared the strikes in the various local coal fields to be a national strike, and he called for strike action from all NUM members. Miners in South Wales, Yorkshire, Kent, Scotland and South Wales all supported this call. But those in North Wales and the Midlands were less convinced.

The Nottinghamshire NUM disagreed with his call for a national strike without a national ballot, and urged for one to take place. The Notts coal field was the second biggest in Britain, only behind Yorkshire in the numbers it employed, and it had benefited from recent modernisation and still held large coal reserves.

Whilst 20% of the Notts miners took immediate strike action, just as Scargill requested, the rest followed the stance of their local NUM. They awaited a national ballot to determine what further action was required.

This was now leading miners from Yorkshire to picket at the Nottinghamshire pits, increasing the tension and resentment amongst the miners themselves.

But for us, this was just newspaper talk. We weren't even in the country, and we had a train to catch. Along with the rest of the Forest lads we'd met in Ostend, we aimed to catch the late morning train to Brussels. We were now moving camp to the Belgian capital.

We woke, dressed and went down for breakfast. Ginger Gary and Bridget left us to rejoin the lads they'd travelled over with, and told us they'd see us later.

Breakfast's topic of conversation centred on the unknown whereabouts of Crazy Till, who was still absent from the previous night. He had last been seen in a disco with a bunch of young ladies from Leeds. However, the smart money wasn't on him still being with them now.

We all put forward various opinions as to where he might be and what might have happened. But truth be told, we didn't have a clue.

The only problem would be if he wasn't back when it was time for us to catch the train.

After eating we went back to our room for the last time. We began packing our bags ready to move on to Brussels.

"Do you think we should pack Till's bag for him?" asked Webby.

"No, I'll do it myself mate, cheers!" said a smiling Till, walking into the room and looking really pleased with himself.

"Where the fuck have you been mate?" I asked, beating the rest to ask the question we were all thinking.

"I got nicked last night," he said. "Me and Eddie!"

"What are you looking so happy about then?" DD asked him, noting the grin that hadn't left his face since his return.

"They've let me go," Till said. "No charges!"

The questions continued – and from what Till could actually remember, it sounded like he'd been pissed up, started messing around, and got nicked for being in the wrong place at the wrong time.

We checked out of the hotel and made our way to the train station.

It was another warm day in Belgium and we enjoyed a stroll through the sunny streets, arriving at the station in plenty of time to buy our tickets and make our way onto the platform for the train. The train was already in, so we boarded it. We found ourselves a carriage, next to two

9. THE GREAT TRAIN ROBBERY

others that were already full of the Forest fans we had spent much of the previous day with. Some more Reds got on the train, which was now pretty much full and was now only a couple of minutes from its scheduled departure time.

Compared to the 'football specials' that British Rail kindly put on for our usual away day excursions, this was a far more comfortable and a far more modern train – complete with spotless toilets and seating that wasn't stained nor ripped beyond repair.

Unlike British Rail, the train also left Ostend bang on time, pulling out of the station and kicking us off on the next leg of our journey.

We were also delighted to find there was a buffet car on the train, meaning we would be able to get some refreshments as we travelled through the Belgian countryside.

What we didn't immediately realise, but soon found out, was that there would be a steward going from carriage to carriage, serving the food and drink from a large trolley. Thus saving us passengers from even having to leave our seats to go down to the buffet car.

Having already had breakfast none of us were too bothered about any more food at this time. So we just settled down in our carriage, laughing and joking – speculating on what delights Brussels might hold in store.

Till was the exception. Having missed breakfast, he was still hungry but had a dilemma.

"I'm starving," he said, "but I've not got much money left and I don't want to waste it on food!"

"Just about sums it up!" said Webby. "I'm running low as well!"

DD was about to speak when Scrawn interrupted him.

"Look at this!" he said, motioning for us to look out of our carriage and along the train corridor.

We looked, and saw that the steward and his refreshment trolley had now reached the carriages next to us that were full of Forest fans. As he went into one carriage to take the orders of the lads in there, fans from the other carriage were helping themselves off his trolley.

The steward would then return to his trolley, get the stuff that had been ordered and go back in to the carriage to deliver it – and more stuff would be pinched. This whole process was then being repeated again as he went into the next carriage and so on.

"Bloody hell, you're not telling me that he's not noticed how much stuffs gone missing!" I said, wondering why he hadn't done something about it.

"He knows," said Scrawn, "but what's he going to do about it?" That summed up the helpless situation the steward had found himself in.

The steward then entered in to our carriage,

"Sandwiches, soda, coffee, chocolate," he started. Then he ended prematurely, presumably aware that we weren't really listening to him. Our distraction was being caused by the robbing of his trolley, going on behind his back.

We all declined any beverages, leaving the steward free to return to rescue his trolley and whatever contents still remained.

As he moved along to the next carriage, he pulled his trolley further up the train corridor. Eddie, one of the Forest fans, was now crawling on his hands and knees behind it, taking cans of drink off the bottom shelf of the refreshment trolley even as it was moving along.

"Now that is taking the piss!" said DD, but we all still had to giggle.

It wasn't too long after that when the ticket inspector entered into our carriage. Once he had checked and stamped our tickets, he moved to do the same in the next carriages.

Shortly afterwards, the train pulled into Brugge station. This presented an opportunity for us to peer out the windows and have a bit of a look around. A few passengers got off, but surprisingly few got on. There was the odd shout of "Forest" and "You Reds!" out of the windows as we waited to pull out the station.

9. THE GREAT TRAIN ROBBERY

Only we didn't pull out of the station. We seemed to have come to a halt.

The train remained stationary for some time, leading us to believe that something was amiss.

"What's going on here?" wondered Webby. He pointed out of the window, to where the ticket inspector was heading off the train and into the station.

He was followed into the station by another member of the train's staff, raising concerns amongst us as to what was taking place.

"Could be the end of their shift?" I suggested, but I was just guessing.

"Or maybe they just need a piss?" said one of the other Forest lads, with everyone now looking on and wondering exactly what was happening.

Whilst people's speculations began to range from the bizarre to the insane, we all shared one thing: worry. Something wasn't right.

"Here they are!" someone eventually noted, spotting the two rail staff as they both made their way back on board the train.

"Hooray!!" the cheer went up. And once again the train set off, up and running.

"Don't some people panic?" said Scrawn, as if there had never been any reason for concern.

In truth I had been worried, and I'd noted a level of anxiety amongst most of the other Forest lads whilst the train was being delayed. But now we were underway, most of them were looking relaxed again.

"Right, I'm going for a shave," said Scrawn, looking to repeat his achievement when we had travelled down to Dover. He grabbed his wash-bag and headed down the train to the toilet.

"Ghent!" said Webby, alerting us all that we had arrived at the next port of call.

The train came to a halt, and more passengers left the train at Ghent station. As I watched them depart, I noticed that some of the Forest fans in the furthest carriage were getting up to leave. Before I could work out why they would want to get off at Ghent, I realised they weren't; they were all seemingly moving to another carriage.

Some of the lads in the next carriage started to do the same, and I began to wonder what was really going on. Then, just as a few of them moved into our carriage, I understood what the fuss was about. It was the police.

The police were boarding the train and there were loads of them.

They started to go from carriage to carriage, and they were targeting the Forest fans. A lad ran past our carriage. As he did so, he discarded a knife. It slid along the floor of our carriage, and landed right between mine and DD's feet. Fucking shit!!

"Passports!" the police demanded, as they entered the next carriage to us. We had to move fast. Next second they would be here!

I went to back-kick the knife under the seat. But as I lifted my foot to do so, a hand reached out from under my seat and grabbed the knife, moving it out of sight.

"Passports!" The police were now in our carriage.

My head still hadn't accepted that someone was actually lying underneath the seats that me and DD were sitting on. I'd had no idea they were there. And now the police were in our carriage, demanding our passports. They would presumably be more than a little interested to find the knife that two seconds ago, lay in front of me.

The police officers stepped back out of the carriage and waited at the door. They were taking everybody's passports off them, and then herding all the Forest fans together on the station platform. Outside the train there were loads more police, some of whom were dressed in riot gear.

"Passport!" The cop in the doorway of our carriage was fast becoming impatient, and he instructed me to hand mine over to him now.

Kingy, Scrawn and Johnny Woods

Till, Dave Illingworth and Johnny Woods

Tommy, DD, Keith and Parks

Scrawn and Till with others

Webby

Through the Seasons Before Us - Following Nottingham Forest in the 80s

DD

Scrawn's best Tommy impression

Tommy, Scrawn, Parks, Dawesy and Kingy

Kegworth lads at Arsenal in '88

Forest in early '80s

Through the Seasons Before Us - Following Nottingham Forest in the 80s

Forest squad UEFA Cup 83-84 season

My match ticket

9. THE GREAT TRAIN ROBBERY

I grabbed my bag from the luggage rack and pointed behind me, indicating to the copper that my friend had got my passport. I did this in a voice loud enough so that the others could hear me. DD used the same ploy, followed by Webby.

As we left the carriage, the lad who was under our seat – and another who had been hiding under the seat opposite – got up and walked out ahead of Till.

The carriage was now empty, meaning that Till was the last man out. He couldn't use the same ruse as we had. He was forced to hand over his passport, and then explain to the officer that we must have been mistaken; he'd been looking after our passports earlier, but he no longer had them.

This had provided the rest of us with the chance to get off the train with both our bags and our passports.

"They've got Till," Webby said.

"I know, but they've not got us yet," I said. "Run!"

Webby, DD and me all started to leg it down the platform, and another couple of Forest fans had the same idea. We all ran out the station – us three one way, the other lads in the opposite direction. We just kept running and running.

"Stop!" said Webby... knackered, but right in his assessment that nobody had even bothered to chase us and that we were safe.

"OK, let's go and get a drink and have a think." Well, at least that was my plan. I wasn't sure how, but we still had to get to Brussels.

We found a nice quiet bar about half a mile from the train station, where we ordered a round of drinks and sat down. We began to discuss our options and consider the current situation.

Scrawn, we assumed, would still be on the train – having timed to perfection his trip to the toilet to have a shave. Till must have been apprehended by the cops, we had witnessed that much with our own eyes. What would happen to him now was anybody's guess.

"We can't do anything about Till," I said. "He may have been arrested, deported or just thrown in the cells for a while. We just don't know."

"But Scrawn's still on the train, so we need to get to Brussels and try to find him!"

"It's not going to be easy finding Scrawn in a great big place like Brussels!" DD rightly pointed out. "It was hard enough in Ostend!"

"First job is to get to Brussels, we can't do anything until then," Webby said, reminding us of our primary objective.

Our options were limited. We couldn't drive, it was too far to walk and there was not much chance of the three of us being able to hitch a lift.

That left catching either the bus or the train as the only means to reach our destination, we reasoned.

"We've already got train tickets," Webby said, and continued by reminding us that he hadn't got much money left.

DD agreed; the train was our best option. The only problem was, we didn't know if the police would still be at the station or even if they were still looking for us. It was a risk. But we had few, if any, alternatives.

"We all need to change our clothes," I said, explaining that if we got stopped, we'd deny even being on the train. We'd say that we'd been staying in Ghent and we were going to Brussels to see friends, not for the football.

We walked back to the station through what looked to be a picturesque town, bracing ourselves for what we might find waiting for us there.

We gained access to the platform via the main entrance, and didn't see any police officers anywhere. It had only been an hour since we'd been here before so we all remained tense and alert.

Lady Luck was smiling on us, and continued to do so – as the next train to Brussels was due in only ten minutes' time. We sat quietly, keep-

9. THE GREAT TRAIN ROBBERY

ing our heads down and nervously watching out for any sign of the police.

Our train arrived and we spirited ourselves onto it, heads down and trying to remain invisible. We sat down, maintaining a low profile as best we could. The train started up and we began to think we'd safely made it.

"Shit" I said, no louder than was necessary – highlighting to Webby and DD the large number of police vans that were still parked at the side of the train station. There looked to be at least twelve vans; I started to count, but the train was picking up speed and I ended up having to estimate.

"Bet they've still got them all in the station for questioning," DD said.

It seemed a fair assumption. One that made perfect sense.

"Tickets please," the ticket inspector asked, realising that we were English. We all gave him our tickets. He looked at them closely and asked us why they had already been stamped.

We explained that we had started our journey to Brussels in Ostend, but wanted to stop off in Ghent because everyone had told us what a lovely city it was.

How much of our explanation he understood or believed will never be known. But the end result was that he stamped our tickets once more, and bid us all good day.

It was with great relief that we finally made it to Brussels. We got off the train at the 'Central' station, for no other reason than it being 'middle for diddle'. None of us had been to Brussels before, so we had no prior knowledge. It was a case of just doing the most obvious thing.

We walked up the platform carrying our travel bags, pondering what our next move would be and trying to find our way out of the station.

Shortly before we reached the main exit we heard someone shouting in English.

"Oi!" he shouted again, and this time we all looked around.

Waving at us like crazy and riding down one of the train station's escalators, there he was – Pierre Cardin. Or should I say Crazy Till, still dressed in his not-so-new beige t-shirt!

It was great to see him.

10. DÉJÀ VU

It was typical of Till. The rest of us have to leg it and only just get away from the police, whilst he gets collared yet still manages to arrive in Brussels first. One of life's great survivors, was Till.

He informed us that nobody had actually been arrested in Ghent. The police had identified and searched everybody, before eventually releasing them without any charges. Along with the other lads, Till was put onto the next train to Brussels and he had arrived half hour or so before us.

"How did you know to wait for us at the Central Station?" I asked him.

"Oh, is there more than one station then?" he answered. "I just got off with all the others."

From Till's reply, we now knew that the other lads shouldn't be too far away. So we left the station to scout around some of the bars located nearby. We quickly found some of the lads.

We had a quick drink, and then it was decided that we should get booked into some digs before doing anything else.

One of the lads had noted that there was a Youth Hostel located close to the train station. He suggested it might be a good option for some cheap accommodation. Everyone agreed we should give it a try, there was nothing to lose.

On our arrival at the Youth Hostel there seemed to be a hint of concern shown by the receptionist, as twelve to fifteen of us all piled into the hostel. A few of the lads went out of their way to be as friendly as possible, and did their best to put the receptionist at ease. Because we only required beds for one night, this gave us a better chance of finding a vacancy. The receptionist checked through her books to determine just how many beds were free, and she told us there was room for all of us.

All she required now was for us to show her our Youth Hostelling membership cards, and we were as good as in.

The trouble was: we didn't have one between us.

There followed a lot of negotiating, pleas and excuses – and her initial refusal was skilfully manipulated around, until all of us were allowed to stay. Fortunately for us, a couple of the lads proved to be silver tongued and very persuasive. We all paid our fees and booked in.

The hostel had a lot of different rooms, but our one had eight bunk beds. Most of us were allocated this room, although a couple of the lads were put into elsewhere.

The room was basic, but clean and cheap, making it ideal for what we needed. The only problem was that because it was a communal room, there was little or no security for all our personal belongings. Anyone could get in and steal our stuff.

One of the Forest lads suggested that we should get a locker at the train station. We could keep anything of value locked up there, and just leave our wash-bags and other items of little value in the rooms.

So we all got lockers and stored our valuables at the Central Station. We were now ready to go out and have a few beers.

We had a whole new city to explore. We also faced the small problem of tracking Scrawn down. It all seemed just a little too familiar!

Scrawn had last seen Till being detained by the coppers on the station platform, back in Ghent. He had assumed that the rest of us would most likely have been with him, although he couldn't actually see any of us as he peered out of the train window.

The train had pulled off with the rest of the Forest lads all being kicked off, so he was pretty much on his own for the rest of the journey to Brussels. His arrival in the Belgian capital presented him with the dilemma of what to do next.

10. DÉJÀ VU

He wasn't sure that the cops would release the fans they had detained in Ghent. So should he wait for us? Or try to find other Forest fans?

He chose the latter option, but first he thought he would try and find somewhere to stay.

The centre of Brussels wasn't short of accommodation, but finding somewhere within his price range was a little more difficult. Eventually, after a bit of a walk around various different hotels, Scrawn found somewhere that met his requirements.

However, with uncertainty hanging over whether or not the rest of us would be arriving in Brussels, Scrawn resisted booking into the hotel. He merely checked its availability, explaining that he would return later to book in once his friends arrived.

On his own in the middle of Brussels, Scrawn headed the short distance back towards the railway station and made his way into one of the nearby bars for a drink.

He ordered a beer and sat down in the corner of the room, keeping himself to himself. He had a quick look around the bar. There were a few people in, enjoying an early afternoon drink, but none were faces he knew. He drank his beer and, having seen nobody he recognised, left the bar and headed down the street, hoping to bump into other Forest fans along the way.

He made his way to another bar and tried his luck in there.

He purchased a beer and again sat down to drink it. The bar was not as busy as the previous place, but looking round the room, he saw a couple of faces that seemed familiar to him.

Scrawn nodded to a couple of blokes at a table on the other side of the room. They nodded back, confirming his suspicion that he had seen them before.

He walked across the room to join them. "How are you going on then?" he asked. "When did you get here?"

The lads replied that they had been in Brussels since the day before, and they were waiting for a couple more Forest fans they had arranged to meet in the bar.

The three of them soon numbered five, as the Forest fans they'd arranged to meet finally arrived. And by the time they'd bought another round of beers, five had become eight as more fans had come into the bar.

Scrawn's new friends drank their beers and decided to go for a walkabout, to see what was happening round the town. They walked through the city centre, eventually finding a bar which had another dozen or so Reds supporters inside.

Some of the lads in this bar said they had just come from a nearby square, where most of the Forest fans already in Brussels had gathered. Scrawn thought to himself this would probably be the best place to try to find us, and pencilled it in as his next port of call. But before leaving his newfound friends, he stayed and enjoyed another beer and a bit of a singsong along with the other twenty or so Reds in the bar.

About a dozen of us from the Youth Hostel set off into town for a few beers. The lads with us were not interested in keeping a low profile, and we enjoyed ourselves noisily as we made our way through Brussels looking for a suitable bar.

We didn't have long to wait and entered what appeared to be a lively looking bar for a Tuesday afternoon. There were already quite a few Forest fans in there before we arrived, a couple of lads who had been on our train amongst them. DD got the beers in, and we all joined in with the singing and revelry inside the bar. The news was that there were already hundreds of Forest fans in Brussels, and most of them were mainly hanging out in a square just around the corner!

"We'll have this beer in here, then go and see if we can find Scrawn in the Square that they're on about!" I said, thinking it was the most obvious place he might head for.

10. DÉJÀ VU

Till, DD and Webby agreed, meaning that at least we had a plan of action and somewhere to head for.

The square was literally just around the corner from the bar. Before we got there we decided to stop at a shop and get some food, not having eaten since breakfast.

DD and I both picked up several items each, paid for them and left the shop to eat them. Whilst we did so, Till and Webby had chosen to wait for us near the doorway.

Neither of them purchased anything, but they still left the shop with more to eat than either DD or I did. They'd decided to load their pockets with sweets and chocolate whilst we were getting served.

"I've got no money left for food," Webby said in his defence, explaining his predicament to us. Till just laughed.

We reached the square and immediately noticed a large group of lads. They were all sat at tables outside a couple of bars down one side of the square.

There were about sixty to eighty Forest fans scattered around this area, many of whom I knew.

We headed into one of the bars to get some more drinks and bingo – there, already standing at the bar, was Scrawn.

It had only been two days since we had searched all over Ostend for him. Now we had repeated the same task in Brussels, with the same result: again we were reunited.

"Good to see you lads!" said Scrawn. "I didn't know what had happened to you, back in Ghent."

We explained our tale and quickly brought him up to speed with the course of events. We finished by telling him that we'd booked into a Youth Hostel near the Central station.

"That's good enough for me. I'll stay there as well then," Scrawn told us.

So whilst Webby, Till and me had a couple more drinks in the square,

Scrawn went off with DD to put his bag into DD's locker at the train station.

They quickly rejoined us, and we spent the rest of the afternoon and early evening sat outside in the square – having a laugh and watching the world go by with the rest of the Forest fans.

As we sat in the square, having a drink and enjoying ourselves, we noticed a group of five or six lads keeping themselves to the fringes of our gathering. What made them stand out was the fact they were almost all identically attired: jeans and green flight jackets.

Four or five years earlier, they would have fitted right in. But times had changed and now they stuck out like sore thumbs.

After a while, they approached some of the Forest lads and began talking to them. They told the Forest lads that they were supporters of KV Mechelen, and that they hated Anderlecht. As such, they said they wanted to join up with Forest to fight against Anderlecht at tomorrow's match. From what they said, there were supposedly forty or fifty Mechelen fans who wanted to fight alongside Forest.

Some of the Forest lads seemed to accept the idea, but most were set against it. In fact one plan put forward was to welcome the Mechelen fans, then ambush them.

In the end, I think the Mechelen fans could see for themselves that they wouldn't be too welcome and had a rethink.

As the evening progressed, small groups of lads were starting to wander off to do their own thing. But for the time being, we remained in the square with the lads we had been in Ostend with.

DD took time out from drinking to go for a much needed slash.

He stuffed his baguette into his back pocket, deeming it a safer option than leaving it on his table where we were all sat.

Whilst in the toilets, Bridget and three locals were in the urinals at the same time.

10. DÉJÀ VU

"How are you getting on mate," Bridget said, acknowledging DD.

"OK cheers," came DD's reply.

DD had just about finished his piss when he heard Bridget say, "Right lads, let's be having you!"

With this, he rounded on the three locals and waded in to them like a whirlwind – uprooting them and leaving them reeling.

DD returned to our table, munching on his baguette.

"You'll not believe what's just happened in there!" he said, telling us the tale that he'd just bore witness to.

We now numbered about forty-odd. As the evening progressed the vast majority were in favour of taking a look around Brussels' red light area, as you do.

We all walked briskly through the city centre, quickly reaching the red light area. We soon found ourselves walking down a street full of topless bars, massage parlours and sex shows. The further we walked, the more dispersed our group became – with people stopping off at various points to have a closer look.

By the time we had almost reached the far end of the street, there were only about twenty of us still together in a group, albeit we were now spread out on both sides of the road. As we walked towards a bar at the bottom of the street, we passed yet another massage parlour. A couple of the lads stopped briefly for a quick nosey through the windows, then carried on walking.

Next second, a couple of prostitutes came out of the massage parlour. One of them in particular ran after the lads that had just stopped for a look, chasing them down the road.

"Eh, English! I fuck you, I fuck you!" she screamed, scaring the bejesus out of them and making the rest of us laugh our heads off.

Our laughter was short lived. The prostitute didn't take too kindly to us laughing at her, and she rounded on anyone who was near her.

"English I fuck you all!" she screamed – and if she could have caught any of us, she probably would have done!

When we finally reached the bar we were headed for, we found a warm welcome even though there was a large group of us.

We made our way to the bar and it soon become obvious why we were made so welcome.

"How much?" Till exclaimed. "I'm not paying that!"

We realised the beer was going to be expensive, but the price they wanted was totally ridiculous.

"I am not bothered about staying in here, it's a rip-off," I chipped into the conversation. Webby and DD agreed, leaving just Scrawn out of the five of us willing to stay.

"We'll find another bar and meet you later then mate," DD said. So Till, Webby, DD and me all left the pub.

Three or four other lads also made the same choice, and all of us set off to find a more reasonably priced bar.

Every bar in the red light area was going to be expensive, so we were forced to wander a little further afield. Despite our efforts, we couldn't find one anywhere. The other lads decided they would keep searching, but the four of us gave up and headed back to meet up with Scrawn.

When we returned to the bar where Scrawn was drinking, most of the Forest lads were still inside. We waited in the street, chatting with a couple of lads who'd already had enough and come outside.

One of the lads, who was from the South Coast, decided it was time for some gentle exercise. He walked a few yards down a nearby side-street, and single handed started trying to roll a Citroen CV over onto its side. He picked it up and almost had it toppling over, only just falling short of success. He had another go, then another – each time only failing by the narrowest of margins. Eventually he gave up and rejoined us, chatting away quite normally as if nothing had happened. Mid-conversation,

10. DÉJÀ VU

he mentioned that of all the other teams, it was only Southampton and Derby that he really hated. This was of some interest to Till and Webby, who decided that it would be better if they kept their distance from him after that.

"We're going to have a quick look around, see what's happening," Till said. And with that, he and Webby made their way back up the street and disappeared into one of the strip bars.

"What are they on with now," DD asked, shaking his head. "They've got no money, they're going to end up getting a good hiding!"

Scrawn came out the bar with a few more of the others, just in time to catch the end of our conversation. He too shook his head, more in disdain than disbelief.

We set off back up the street, looking through the windows of the bar that Till and Webby had disappeared into. There was no sign of either of them, so we continued on our way.

"We had better wait here for them," I said, after we'd made it back to the top end of the street, nearer to the square.

After waiting there for a minute or so, we saw Till and Webby come out of the bar they had been in. They walked no more than ten yards before they stopped outside a massage parlour, had a quick look, then popped inside. As we wondered what they were on with now, they were back out. They then crossed the road and sauntered straight into another topless bar.

"They've got no money," I reasoned to DD and Scrawn.

"Try telling that pair!" DD replied, adding prophetically, "It's going to be a long night!"

Seconds later and Till and Webby remerged, only to walk a few yards back towards us before diving into yet another bar. This pattern continued for almost half an hour. We watched them zigzag their way back to where we were waiting for them at the top of the road. It was quite amusing.

The two of them were both completely oblivious to everything else going on in the world. They had become completely seduced by the thrills and sights of Brussels red light district.

Trouble for them was that they had no money.

This made them nuisances rather than customers – which meant they were reduced to popping into every bar, massage parlour and sex show along the street to witness whatever cheap thrills they could see, before being told to leave. They certainly got their money's worth!

Eventually, they spotted us and rejoined us rather sheepishly.

"Did you enjoy that?" DD asked them, leaving both Till and Webby a little lost for words.

"Was there anywhere that you didn't go in?" asked Scrawn, which was a fair question after what we had just seen.

"How long have you been stood here watching us?" questioned Webby, realising that their little jaunt had not gone unnoticed.

"Long enough," we replied. "Long enough!"

It was still fairly early when we arrived back at the Youth Hostel. We had stopped for a drink on the way, but just had the one. We got Scrawn into the hostel with no problems whatsoever. He even managed to get himself a bunk-bed – which was more than DD did, and he was already booked in!

I had the top bunk above Webby, with DD underneath us on the floor. Scrawn and Till also had bunks in the same dorm.

As well as the Forest lads, there were a few other guests staying in the same room as us. Most of them were already tucked up in bed when we arrived back. The majority of the Forest fans were still out around town.

It had again been another action-packed day, and I reflected upon its events as my head hit the pillow. I settled down for some well-deserved sleep, playing the day back to myself in my head.

10. DÉJÀ VU

There had been our little detour in Ghent after the police had raided our train, the search for Scrawn again, the afternoon we had spent in the square, and finally Webby and Till's determined but fruitless search for cheap sex. All in all, another memorable day... one which was now fading as I drifted into sleep.

Feeling totally disorientated I awoke in the middle of the night to see half a dozen of the Forest lads accompanied by a load of giggling women, all of them wandering around the dormitory. I was still half asleep – the noise of their laughing and joking had woken me, but my wits and senses were yet barely functional. Then just as quickly as they had come in to the dorm, they were gone.

"Did you see that?" Webby asked.

"Yeah," said DD, "Where do you reckon they're going now?"

It was a question that remained unanswered. Despite our excitement, it remained daft o'clock in the early hours of the morning, and we were just too knackered to be bothered to do anything much about it.

11. WHEN TWO TRIBES GO TO WAR

Wednesday 25th April 1984. This was the day which would decide whether or not Forest would play in the UEFA Cup Final.

Today was the real reason for our trip. But unfortunately it was the day that Scrawn was to return home, and would miss the match.

With so many people in the dormitory, there was a lot of activity going on. For a light sleeper like me, there was no chance of sleeping in late.

As it happened, pretty much everybody was soon awake and the five of us Kegworth lads decided to go out to get some breakfast.

We got out of bed and started to get dressed. To everyone's astonishment, Till decided not to wear his Pierre Cardin t-shirt.

"Blimey, I didn't know that shirt came off Till," DD taunted him. But Till took no notice, he was too busy checking out his Fila track suit top in the mirror.

Webby followed suit. He also wore a track suit top, a pale blue Ellesse one that he wore over a new yellow Pringle jumper. It didn't just feel like match day, it now started to look like match day too.

It was at this point that DD dropped a bit of a bombshell. He told us that he would have to go back with Scrawn, because he too had run out of money.

"We've got no money either," said Till, referring to himself and Webby. "But we're going to stay for the match. It's what we've all come for!"

"I haven't even got the money for a ticket," said DD. "I'm totally skint!"

Despite them having no money left, both Webby and Till had given me enough to get them a match ticket a couple of days earlier. In doing so, they had made sure they wouldn't spend it and have to miss the game.

It looked like it would be just the three of us at the match.

We arrived at a shop that seemed like a cross between a bakery and a sandwich shop. The ideal place for us to get our breakfast.

We went into the shop and had a look around. DD and Scrawn both decided to buy some baguettes, whilst I chose some croissants and fruit. Once again Till and Webby stuck to their staple diet of chocolate and sweets, utilising the 'self-service' method they were now close to perfecting.

We ate our breakfast as we slowly walked back to the hostel.

"What time are you going to be leaving?" I asked Scrawn.

"We've got to leave by 10.30am to get to Ostend in time to catch the Ferry."

That didn't leave them long to get to the Youth Hostel, pack their bags and then catch the train. When we arrived back, a couple of the lads told us that they were going to go down to Anderlecht's ground to buy some tickets for the game. I gave them our money and asked them to get three tickets for Webby, Till and myself.

We said our reluctant goodbyes to DD and Scrawn and wished them a safe journey, saying we'd meet them back at the house in London on Thursday. Then we checked out of the hostel and left with the other Forest lads, to make our way back to the square and meet up with everyone.

Scrawn and DD were soon packed and ready to leave. The once busy dorm that had been bustling with activity all morning was now silent and empty, except for the pair of them. Their loneliness reinforced the sad truth that they now had to part company with our adventure and set sail for home. It was not the ending they had envisaged a few days earlier.

"Come on," said Scrawn, trying to salvage something from their predicament. "Let's go and have a look around."

11. WHEN TWO TRIBES GO TO WAR

The pair of them grabbed their bags and explored the rest of the hostel.

Just like the dorm they'd stayed in, the other rooms were now also deserted. The people staying there had already gone out for the day.

They went room to room, looking for anything that may have been discarded by the other guests. In one dormitory Scrawn found a cream Tony Curtis-style leather jacket, and liberated it from the wardrobe that had imprisoned it.

Nothing else was forthcoming, and they left the hostel to catch the train back to Ostend – still feeling as if they were getting off a rollercoaster half way through the ride.

The square was already full of Forest fans, and it still wasn't quite midday. The lads who had gone to fetch our match tickets from the ground had returned and distributed the tickets.

The excitement was growing, and the atmosphere in the square continued to build as the beer began to flow once again. Forest songs were being sung loudly, attracting the attention of people who were passing by. Cars were honking their horns, and our flags and banners were now flying high in the square.

Talk began to turn towards the game. The mood amongst the fans was one of confidence, rightly so with Forest two – nil up from the first leg.

We spent a couple of hours in the square – soaking up the atmosphere, having a couple of beers and enjoying ourselves. By mid-afternoon, a lot of the lads we had been with for the past few days said they were going for a drink at the bars around the ground. So along with many more Forest fans, we left the square and headed towards the football ground.

It was a couple of miles from the square in the centre of Brussels to the ground where Anderlecht were playing. We all headed to the tram stop and utilised the capital's public transport system to shorten our journey time.

Whilst on the tram, the atmosphere created in the square was once again evident, and the non-football passengers were treated to a wide range of Forest songs as we made our way through the city. The tram was heaving, with loads of Forest fans crammed tightly into every available space.

Instinctively, the song *We all hate Rams* was transformed to *We all hate trams*. Not exactly Joe Strummer, but it was witty enough to keep us all amused for a little while.

We had got half way to the stadium when we pulled into one of the many tram stops along the route. At the stop, there were four or five teenage Anderlecht fans waiting for the tram. As the doors opened, they realised that it was completely full of Forest fans, so they started to shout at us and one of them even had the bottle to give us the finger!

A couple of the Forest lads got up, jumped off the tram and jokingly pretended to chase after the young Anderlecht fans, much to everybody's amusement.

But just as soon as they'd got off, the doors closed behind them and the tram pulled away from the stop. Despite them only going five or six yards away from the tram, the two lads were being left behind and it was now their misfortune that we were all laughing at!

Pretty soon we had arrived at the stop nearest the ground. Everyone got off, and we made our way towards the stadium. There was already a large police presence around – albeit one that seemed prepared to keep a low profile, for the time being at least. The majority of the supporters who had arrived early at the ground were Forest fans, not surprising given that it was the middle of the afternoon and most Anderlecht fans would still be at work.

Webby, Till and I went for a walk round the outside of the ground, noting where we would be standing and which way we needed to go to find our way back to the tram stop after the match.

11. WHEN TWO TRIBES GO TO WAR

We circumnavigated the stadium, going almost full circle to where the majority of Forest fans were gathered. We entered a bar and I bought a round of drinks for Webby, Till and myself. Then we stood outside with scores of other Forest fans.

All the time, more and more fans were arriving. People travelling by car, train, bus and airplane were arriving at the ground – having made the trip hoping to see Forest progress to the UEFA Cup Final.

For a lot of the fans, it was a short one- or two-day trip that entailed spending hours travelling to the game, seeing the match and then taking hours to get back home. For many, that was the European away day experience. Fortunately for us, we had taken a different approach and we had already experienced enough adventures to be able to write a book!

As more Forest fans arrived, there were many familiar faces. Forest fans I knew from various games, and others we knew from evenings out around town.

Till's mate Gilly spotted him amidst the crowds of fans, and came over to us for a chat. He'd literally only just got off his coach but was already pissed, thanks to an endless supply of beer on the bus and then on the ferry.

I went inside to get us some more beers, but by now the bar was so full that getting served looked like being a long job. I thought it would be easier to try and find another bar, where we would get served quicker.

I went back outside and told Till and Webby what the crack was. They agreed we should make a move, and try to find somewhere else. Gilly said he would see us later, and he left us to return to the mates he'd travelled over with.

We only had to walk fifty yards or so before we saw what looked to be another large group of Forest fans, stood outside the football ground.

"There must be another bar over there!" Webby said, pointing towards the group of people. "Let's go over and take a look."

We walked the remaining forty yards to where they were all gathered, and started to hear the football songs that were being sung. But it was only when we got nearer that we realised there were, in fact, two groups of fans: one Forest, and the other Anderlecht.

It was also evident there was a large police presence, something that had not been immediately apparent.

The police had formed a line across the full width of the road – separating the two sets of supporters, keeping them apart. The police officers in the line were all wearing full riot gear, which was a contrast to the way most of the police we had seen so far had been dressed.

We looked around but there was no sign of any bars, or anywhere else to get a drink from.

"What we doing then?" Webby asked. "Are we bothering with another drink?"

Just as he spoke, a brick flew through the air. It was coming towards us, straight in our direction. It landed short, but once it had hit the ground it bounced on and hit Webby on his leg.

"Bastards!" said one of the Forest lads just in front of us, who had only narrowly avoided wearing the brick on his head. "That was bloody close, I didn't even see it!"

"How long's all this been going on?" asked Till.

"They've been stood behind the coppers, chucking stuff for about fifteen minutes or so. The coppers seem happy to let them do it," he told us.

I looked about. There seemed to be about seventy Forest fans and maybe an hundred or so Anderlecht fans behind the line of police. But both groups of fans were growing all the time.

We were only a hundred yards or so from the bar we had just left, where most of the Forest fans were drinking. Some of those supporters were now inevitably leaving the bar, to join the growing number of fans on our side of the police line.

11. WHEN TWO TRIBES GO TO WAR

Many of the lads we'd spent most of our time with in Ostend and Brussels were among the fans now arriving.

There were also a few Uttrecht fans with us. They had previously attended Forest's game in Holland against PSV in an earlier round. The reason for this was that they wanted to show their support for Forest's Dutch goalkeeper, Hans Van Breukelen, who used to play for Uttrecht.

The Anderlecht fans continued to chant at us from behind the police line. With their numbers also swelling, so did their confidence – and yet another barrage of missiles was thrown in our direction.

Once again the police seemed content that this should be allowed to happen, and they took no action to try to stop the Anderlecht fans.

That was the final straw for many of the Forest fans. One lad with blood streaming from his head began remonstrating with the police to do something about it. Some of his mates were supporting him, and they began to argue and jostle with the police.

At exactly the same time, a hardcore group of Forest lads charged headlong into the other side of the police line. It splintered, allowing scores of Forest to pour through the gaps and reach where the Anderlecht fans stood.

It was like the start of the Grand National as the Belgians ran in every possible direction – they didn't seem so brave now!

The police regrouped very quickly, moving to once again separate the two factions. They reformed their line across the street, restoring order.

Three or four Forest lads were caught on the wrong side of the police line. They began to take a bit of a pasting from the Anderlecht fans, once they had regrouped. Still the police seemed to do nothing, looking on whilst the Forest lads were assaulted.

This continued until one of the Forest lads was beaten unconscious. He lay in the middle of the road, a bloody and lifeless mess.

A roar went up, and once again scores of outraged Forest fans charged straight at the police line. This time the police didn't just buckle, some of them actually ran!

We were through their line in an instant, now charging down the road to rescue the trapped and isolated Forest fans.

Retribution was swift and the few Anderlecht fans that initially stood their ground didn't fare well. They succumbed to the sheer weight of our numbers or just took to their toes. It was all over very quickly. Just as well – because once the police had finally regrouped, they started hitting out at anyone they could find.

The Forest fans briskly returned to the top end of the street, where we had started. The police line yet again reformed in our wake.

Till was now wearing an Anderlecht floppy hat, along with the broadest smile, when he and me returned to where Webby was waiting for us.

"It's a trophy, isn't it!" he said, beaming with pride.

It was only now that I noticed the Belgian police were deploying 'snatch squads', out of police jeeps. These officers were not dressed in full riot gear; they wore sweaters, combat trousers, boots and a beret. They seemed to collectively identify a target, then jump out their jeep, arrest him and drag him off to be put inside a police van.

In the space of a few minutes, several high-profile Forest lads were nicked in this fashion – including a couple we knew from our time in Ostend.

This put the police a little more in control, and things started to calm down a bit. In turn, it encouraged the Anderlecht fans to start up their chants again, but this time they wisely refrained from chucking anything else in our direction.

"Come on, let's have a walk back around the ground, it's not that long to kick-off," I said to Webby and Till.

11. WHEN TWO TRIBES GO TO WAR

"It's already kicked-off!" Till said, adding, "Oh, you mean the match!"

We took a slow walk back around the ground, along with many other supporters. Most fans were starting to make their way into the stadium.

The stadium itself was of reasonable size, with a circa 38,000 capacity.

A rebuilding program had started the previous year, with the intention to have seats all around the ground – apart from at either end, where there would be terraces for standing.

This was pretty much how it currently was. Although not all the seats were in place yet, and some of the construction around the ground seemed to be temporary.

We were stood with the majority of Forest fans, at the opposite end of the ground from the Anderlecht fans we had fought with earlier. The terrace area at our end was split 50/50 with more Anderlecht fans, with what looked to be only a chest high fence separating each faction.

For a new ground, it didn't look that impressive. After making our way through the turnstiles and onto the terrace, we saw the section we had entered was already pretty much full.

It was by far the most crowded part of the entire ground, whilst the section next to us was half empty.

"Come on," I said, "we're going in there."

I pointed towards the adjacent section. It was already mostly full of Forest fans, many of whom – like us – had spilled over from the packed terrace section where they had entered the ground. To get into it we climbed over a fence that was no more than waist high. In the build-up to the game hundreds more Forest fans did the same thing, until we probably had the two most populated sections of the ground.

Ten minutes or so before kick-off, a group of Forest fans began to covertly climb over the next fence and into the next section. Again it was largely the lads we had been with in Ostend, along with other members of Forest's mob. One after another, they climbed over the fence into the next section, which had supposedly been reserved for the Anderlecht supporters.

"Let's go!" said Till, and he was over the fence in a jiffy.

I looked at Webby, and could tell straight away that he didn't seem anywhere near as keen.

"Wait for us here then mate, we'll meet you back here by the end of the game," I told him. Then I followed Crazy Till over the fence.

Looking around, I estimated that maybe eighty or more Forest lads stood behind the goal at the top of the terracing. There were a couple of much smaller groups of Forest fans in there as well. We stood with one group that numbered only half a dozen, including Till and me.

The Anderlecht fans in our section were not all hooligans, far from it. But as you would expect in the terrace next to the away supporters, there were still a fair few of their lads among them.

The Anderlecht supporters at the far end of the ground were now in full voice. They were flying an impressive array of flags and banners, as the atmosphere built up in anticipation of the teams coming out onto the pitch. The Forest fans responded in kind – belting out our songs, adding further to the atmosphere and intensity of the occasion.

Our section was singing too, with both us and the Anderlecht fans displaying enough passion and fervour to match anywhere else inside the ground. There was now a barrage of noise coming from all corners of the stadium. Just as it seemed to peak, the teams emerged from the tunnel and somehow took it to a whole new level!

With the players all out onto the pitch, the noise eventually dropped enough that you could actually hear the fans of both sides chanting. The atmosphere was super-charged. Our anticipation of the match was all but over, it was finally about to kick-off.

My mind wandered and out of nowhere, I thought of how much Scrawn would have loved to have been here; for the match, for the whole day.

11. WHEN TWO TRIBES GO TO WAR

He'll be watching the highlights later on the television, I thought to myself. I just hope that we're both going to be happy with the result.

"Come on you Reds!" I shouted, for Scrawn in his absence.

12. 72 HOURS LATER

Scrawn kept looking at his passport, staring at its date of expiry and shaking his head. He gave a rueful smile and put it back in his pocket. He was gutted, but he knew that he only had himself to blame.

His 72-hour pass was coming to an end, and he boarded the ferry for home at the same time that Webby, Till and me were boarding the tram to take us to the ground.

The only good news on Scrawn's dismal horizon was that DD was accompanying him home, and would provide him with some entertaining company on their journey back to London.

Scrawn was the oldest amongst us on the trip at 24, whilst DD was the youngest at only 18. Yet the two of them were already becoming great friends, often disappearing together with a couple of ladies on our many nights out. Scrawn proudly called DD his 'protégé' or his apprentice. And DD loved acting his part, playing it to the full.

Whether it was on the football pitch, in the pub or on the dance-floor, they would be side by side, feeding off one another. A proper double act.

Now, in the face of adversity – or at least the expiry of the 72-hour pass – they were together once again.

Compared to their outward crossing on the Jetfoil, the ferry back to England was less comfortable and took a lot longer. But it was going to take more than a choppy sea to stop Scrawn and DD making the most of a bad situation, and they set about enjoying themselves on the ferry.

"Can you lend me £20 mate?" DD asked. When he said he was skint, he wasn't joking.

"Yeah, pay me back when you've got it," Scrawn obliged.

"Cheers mate. Right, I'll get the beers in." And off DD toddled towards the bar.

He returned long before Scrawn anticipated him getting served.

DD had a bottle of red wine with him. No glasses for it, just the bottle.

"I wanted lager," Scrawn complained, confused by DD's choice of drink.

"Let's just say that this was cheaper," DD said, ending any such confusion and explaining why they were soon sat down swigging from a bottle of red wine.

The rest of their drinks proved a little more expensive, but they bought them nonetheless. But however many they had, it wouldn't be anywhere near enough to dull the sense of bitter disappointment that engulfed their return journey.

Just as had been the case on the ferry, the train ride back to Victoria Station felt like it was over before it had started.

There seemed to be an air of inevitability about it all.

Everything was closing in. The fat lady was well and truly warming up to close the curtain on Scrawn and DD's holiday adventure. Not even bumping into Leonard Rossiter at Victoria Station could brighten things up.

"Hello Miss Jones!" DD shouted out, in his best 'Rigsby' accent.

It fell on deaf ears. He was ignored by the actor, whilst Scrawn didn't even see him passing by.

A quick tube journey across the capital brought them both back to NW10 in no time at all.

When Scrawn and DD returned to the house where we had stayed the previous Saturday, they were in for a shock. They knocked on the door but were not expecting it to be answered by a woman.

"Can I help you?" she asked, not having the slightest clue as to who either of them were.

Once an explanation had been forthcoming, she invited them in – although she said Steve had told her that his guests would not be returning until Thursday.

12. 72 HOURS LATER

"What's happened?" she asked.

"Long story!" said Scrawn. "But the short version is that my passport was out of date!"

Scrawn went into a little more detail, painful as that was, and the woman was more than happy that his story rang true.

"Steve should be back later, but Howard's still away on business. He's not going to be back until Friday," she explained, putting Scrawn and DD completely in the picture. She invited them to sit down and make themselves at home.

An hour or so later Steve returned home, and he too was more than a little surprised to see them. Once more they explained the reasons why their trip had been cut short.

"Any sign of your lodger?" asked Scrawn.

"Not since Saturday night!" said Steve, with a smile they could all relate to. "Are you lads hungry?"

He told them he was going to get a Chinese later if they fancied it. That seemed like a good call. But first they all settled down, sat back and watched a bit of television, whilst enjoying a nice cup of tea.

It was probably a good idea that Steve went out to fetch the Chinese for their suppers. Fortunately London NW10 didn't have to witness the antics that were a regular occurrence in the Chinese restaurant back in Nowhere City.

Sited just off the marketplace, right in the middle of Kegworth, our local Chinese and its customers were often subjected to a bit of homemade 'entertainment' most weekend nights – usually just after the pubs were closing!

We had invented our own version of British Bulldog, that was played out whilst we waited for our food. The last one to be thrown over the counter was the winner!

Scrawn, who was a big wrestling fan, also used the time whilst he waited for his food, to perfect his 'moves'. More often than not, DD was his unwilling adversary.

The week before we travelled to Belgium, I went in the Chinese late one night to find DD face-down, sprawled on the takeaway's floor. Scrawn was straddled across him, executing his 'surf board' hold.

"Ask him ref, ask him!" Scrawn continuously shouted to nobody in particular, ignoring DD's desperate pleas of submission!

A few seconds later, and Scrawn built on his move. With DD still pinned to the ground, Scrawn now opened the takeaway's door and repeatedly banged it against DD's head!

"Ask him ref!"

DD's screams of submission finally forced the staff to appeal to Scrawn to let him go. He finally obliged, after one final smack of the door against poor DD's head.

Who needed television to entertain you whilst waiting for your food!

Scrawn and DD finished off the Chinese meal that Steve had fetched, and between them they shared a bottle of wine.

"They'll be kicked off now Scrawn," said DD, noting that the Forest game would be underway.

"Don't remind me," said Scrawn, unable to hide his disappointment. They wanted to avoid hearing the score before they could watch the highlights on the television later that night, so that meant killing a few hours before it was due to be transmitted.

DD was flicking through the day's newspaper, whilst Scrawn was busy reading the *Motorcycle News*. Both of them paused when they heard a knock on the door.

Before Steve could answer it, there was another knock. Then he finally opened the door.

"Look, I don't want no more trouble. I just want to collect the rest of my stuff," said Steve's former lodger.

12. 72 HOURS LATER

"Who's this then?" asked Steve, asking who the guy with the lodger was.

"He's just come to give me a hand!"

Steve deliberated. Finally he opened the door to let them both in.

Scrawn and DD had overheard enough of the conversation to know that the lodger had returned. It had given them a warning before he entered the room.

They weren't expecting that the lodger had come back to get his belongings accompanied by a six foot six inch Rastafarian.

The Rasta filled the doorway as he walked into the room. He went over to a vacant chair and sat down opposite Scrawn and DD.

He nodded towards Scrawn, who acknowledged him, nodding back. But not a word passed between them.

"Get your stuff," the Rasta said, giving the go-ahead to his companion.

The lodger then entered the room, with a suitcase in one hand and a bag in the other. He started gathering all his belongings, filling his bags.

He spotted Scrawn immediately, and he started shaking like a leaf – continually glancing over in Scrawn's direction whilst reclaiming his stuff.

But it wasn't the lodger packing his bags that had grabbed Scrawn and DD's attention. It was the big knife that the Rasta had got tucked into the waistband of his trousers.

As the lodger collected together the last of his belongings, he nervously spoke to the Rasta, stuttering as he did so.

"He's the bottle boy!" he said – indicating that Scrawn had been the one that had hit him over the head, though it had been with an ashtray and not a bottle as he had wrongly assumed.

The Rasta heard him, but did nothing. He let it go, and remained seated until the ex-lodger had filled his bags and was ready to leave.

Steve escorted them both out of the house, and the visit finished without any real incident.

"Phew!" DD was relieved to see the back of them, and didn't mind admitting it.

Scrawn picked up his *Motorcycle News* and began to read it again. Uncovering the wine bottle they'd drank earlier, which he'd placed on his lap and covered with his paper... just in case!

After seeing them off the premises, Steve returned to the room. He was a little more shaken than either DD or Scrawn, but nevertheless pleased that their troublesome lodger was now gone. Once and for all, he had finally moved out of the house with no reason to ever come back. Steve fetched them a can of beer each, and the three of them celebrated his departure. The Forest match was now over. They all wondered if the Reds had done enough to reach the final.

There was only one way they were going to find out. So they settled into their chairs to watch the game on the television.

Scrawn knew that with the match now over, we would already be on our way back to Ostend to catch the ferry.

Would we be commiserating or celebrating?

He wouldn't know the answer to that until he had watched the highlights. The one thing that he was absolutely sure about was that he'd much rather have been with us at the match than having to watch it on the box.

He felt sick.

13. MORE THAN JUST A GAME

1. Hans Van Breukelen
2. Viv Anderson
3. Kenny Swain
4. Chris Fairclough
5. Paul Hart
6. Ian Bowyer
7. Steve Wigley
8. Gary Mills
9. Peter Davenport
10. Steve Hodge
11. Colin Walsh
Sub Gary Birtles.

This was the team picked by Brian Clough to represent Nottingham Forest in Anderlecht. This was the team on which we now pinned our hopes of getting into the UEFA Cup Final.

It was not the strongest team that Forest had fielded in recent times, quite ordinary compared to the team that had retained the European Cup only a few years earlier. But it was nevertheless a team that had proved itself good enough to reach this stage of the UEFA Cup.

Teams like Bayern Munich, Real Madrid and Inter Milan had already been knocked out of the competition. Additionally, this Forest team had already also accounted for the likes of PSV Eindhoven and Glasgow Celtic.

The time had come to add Anderlecht – the then-reigning UEFA Cup holders – to our bunch of scalps. We all hoped that our two-goal advantage from the first leg would provide us with the springboard to do so.

The game kicked off, with Forest attacking the end where we all stood. The great atmosphere continued, with the Forest fans clearly making themselves heard amongst the noise that echoed all around the stadium.

The match started in the same vein as most of the European games I had witnessed; cagey and measured, with each side sounding the other out. When Forest did get the ball, they failed to make any real impression on the game. Anderlecht also laboured a little in the first fifteen minutes. The referee wasn't really helping the game to flow, blowing up for a succession of fouls for next to nothing.

So it came as a massive surprise when, with just short of twenty minutes played, Anderlecht scored. Forest lost the ball in their own half and it was eventually picked up by Scifo, Anderlecht's young star player.

He drifted out wide, before cutting back inside and then shooting from the edge of the penalty area to beat Forest keeper Hans Van Breukelen at his near post.

It was a goal out of nothing and one that I thought that our goalie should have saved, being beaten from a distance at his near post.

"Bastard!" I said, looking over at Till to register my disappointment at us conceding the goal. But he wasn't listening to me, he was already moving off towards the commotion that had just broken out to the left of our terrace.

Most of the Forest lads who were in the same section as us had been stood at the back of the terracing, behind the goal. They now all came charging down the terracing, lashing out and dispersing all the celebrating Anderlecht supporters around them. A few fights broke out, and Till was now heading towards them.

But those scuffles were over even before Till had managed to get there. Although some disorder continued, the fighting was all but done as the Anderlecht lads quickly melted into the rest of the crowd.

13. MORE THAN JUST A GAME

Albeit too late, the police now responded. A large deployment of officers in riot gear entered the terracing behind the goal to restore order, arresting several of the Forest lads and lashing out with their batons at the slightest provocation.

As those arrested were led around the pitch and taken away, Till returned to where I remained standing.

The remainder of the first half passed by with no more goals and no further disorder. Forest seemed to grow into the game a little more. But they had yet to play with any real fluency – although that was in part down to the referee, who still seemed unwilling to let the game flow.

Anderlecht looked dangerous each time they came forward. But Forest seemed reasonably able to cope, apart from the obvious exception of the goal. Half time and it was one – nil on the night, but Forest still carried their overall advantage into the second half.

"We could do with a goal Till," I said.

"Yeah, think you're going to need one," he replied. Then he confidently predicted, "There's going to be more trouble in the second half, whether they score again or not. The Forest lads seem well up for it."

"Do you reckon?" I wasn't so sure, given the large number of police still deployed in our section.

We spent the rest of the half time break talking to the Forest lads who made up the small group we were stood with. They shared Till's view that there could well be more trouble; they thought it was a case of 'when' rather than 'if'.

"It will definitely kick off on the walk back to the station," predicted one of the lads.

"Walk back to the station? That's going to be some walk back to the Central Station mate!" I said. "It's got to be two miles!"

"Central Station?" he said, somewhat confused. "Why would we be going back to Central Station? We're all going back to the one near the ground!"

141

"No mate," I corrected him. "Most of the lads have left their bags and stuff in the lockers at Central."

"They did have," he said, correcting my understanding of the situation, "but they all moved them this morning. Nobody's going back to Central."

"Bloody hell, we've still got our bags there!"

Shit, I thought to myself. The three of us would have to catch a tram full of Anderlecht fans to get back to the station, either that or walk for miles. Even Till didn't fancy the prospect of that too much.

Applause started to ring out around the ground, telling me that the teams were taking to the pitch once again. Out came the players. They quickly assembled, lining up ready to start the second half.

The game was well balanced, but I still felt that an away goal would probably be required. Forest had won away at Glasgow and Eindhoven in earlier rounds, so my confidence remained high as the second half got underway.

Anderlecht were now playing with real purpose, but Forest were containing them well and counter-attacking effectively. The match was now a good open affair. Just short of the hour mark, Anderlecht again attacked down Forest's left flank, but their winger appeared to stand on the ball just as he shaped to take on Forest's left back, Kenny Swain. The winger fell to the ground. Though nobody even appealed, the referee amazingly pointed to the spot: penalty!

"You cheating bastard!" I yelled at the ref. As if he could hear me!

The award of a penalty proved to be the signal for the Forest fans to come surging down the terraces again. They cleared a massive space in their wake, forcing the Anderlecht supporters to flee once more.

This resulted in a violent clash with the riot police, who seemingly hit out indiscriminately at anyone that they believed to be British.

Amidst the disorder, the other Forest fans we were stood with had left us to join the fray. So now it was just Till and me stood together on our own.

13. MORE THAN JUST A GAME

With only the two of us there, a couple of nearby Anderlecht fans turned round and taunted us over the award of the penalty, much to the delight of some of the other Anderlecht standing around us.

The penalty was taken and they scored. The tie was now level on aggregate. The Anderlecht fans celebrated wildly and disorder once again flared within our section – as the Forest fans clashed with the police again, whilst the Anderlecht fans taunted us.

The Anderlecht fans near us enthusiastically celebrated their equalising goal. The two lads who had taunted Till and me over the penalty decision were now cheering furiously in our faces. One of them, a tall well-built chap, was right up in Till's face – screaming his unrestrained delight at Anderlecht's goal.

Bang! Till wasn't having any of that, and he hit the big lad round the side of the head. Straight away the big lad moved to retaliate, grabbing hold of Till and wrestling with him.

I smacked him a couple of times, half watching him, half watching his mate. But his mate quickly lost interest and he backed right off. Now I hit the big lad again, this time forcing him to release Till and cover himself up best as he could. Now Till hit him, and I thought that he'd had enough.

I looked up to see two riot cops coming straight for us, rushing out from amongst the crowds and heading our way. They were no more than just a few yards off.

"Till!" I shouted, alerting him to the danger. And with that I was gone – a short sprint to the fence, which I vaulted straight over and back into the section of predominantly Forest fans. I looked back over my shoulder and saw that Till was fast approaching the fence, but the cops were right behind him.

As Till pulled himself up onto the top of the fence, I thought the cops had him. But he somehow managed to jump down – an instant before a police baton crashed against the fence where he had been perched. We disappeared amidst the Forest fans, thankful that the police didn't follow.

We worked our way through the crowd until we found Webby, where we had arranged to meet him.

"It's looking grim mate," Webby said. "Two – nil down, you'll definitely need a goal now."

"You're not wrong," I said, and for the first time I thought the tie was slipping away from Forest. The Anderlecht crowd was now making all the noise and they too could sense victory was theirs for the taking.

Before we settled back into watching the game, we quickly explained to Webby that the rest of the lads had moved their stuff – meaning that we were just about the only Forest fans who'd be going back to the Central Station after the game.

Webby was surprised but, as he said, there wasn't a lot we could do about it. We decided that we'd get the tram back to the station straight after the game.

As the match continued, it was impossible not to notice the steady stream of Forest lads who had been arrested and were being led around the pitch by the police.

"There's Dave... there's Zico... there's whoever," somebody would say, as the police held another Forest fan.

Needing a goal, Forest now dug in and started to play the best they had done all game. They won more possession and began to create one or two chances, the best of which had us shouting for a penalty when Steve Hodge appeared to be fouled in the box.

But overall the tie was still level on aggregate, and Forest were careful not to over-commit too many players forward. Time was running out and extra time was beckoning.

Just as I was telling Webby that I thought we were heading for extra time, Anderlecht scored again! A good through ball was brilliantly finished. With just a few minutes left, Anderlecht led the tie for the first time.

13. MORE THAN JUST A GAME

It was a body blow. It meant Forest had no more than a couple of minutes to throw everything plus the kitchen sink at them – in search of an away goal that would equalise the tie, and also put Forest through on away goals.

Forest piled on the pressure and purposefully laid siege to the Anderlecht goal, but the Belgians wisely defended in numbers. A barrage of crosses into their box saw the Anderlecht defence begin to creak a little for the first time on the night.

Forest threw men forward in desperation, firing more and more crosses into the box. With only seconds of the match left to play, one of the crosses reached Paul Hart who was totally unmarked. He headed it powerfully into the net!

"Yeesss!!" The Reds fans all around me went mental, but I had to go through my routine of checking for a linesman's flag before celebrating. I'd been caught out and disappointed too many times before.

No flag!

I now went completely mental along with all those around me.

But our joy was short lived.

The referee blew for an Anderlecht free kick – a decision that puzzled the Forest players as much as the supporters.

"What was that disallowed for?" was the question that everyone was asking, and nobody could answer.

The linesman hadn't flagged, so it wasn't offside. Hart clearly headed the ball, not handled it. And he was unmarked, so he couldn't have climbed or pushed anybody. Only the referee could say what he did wrong... because the referee was the only one amongst thirty-odd thousand people who actually thought there had been anything wrong with it!

The ref then blew for full time, and Forest were out of the EUFA Cup – knocked out in the cruellest possible fashion.

14. NUMB

Disappointed didn't come close; I left the ground with Webby and Till straight after the final whistle, feeling completely numb.

Anderlecht's third goal and the disallowed Forest goal were two late blows that would take a while to overcome. But for the moment, we had more pressing concerns. We had to get back to the Brussels Central Station to collect our bags from the lockers, then catch the train to Ostend for the late night ferry.

We drifted of out the ground, along with hundreds of other disconsolate Forest fans. All of us were frustrated and forlorn, less about the night's result than about how it had happened.

Defeat is never easy, but this one left a sour taste.

Weaving in-between the crowds, we got to the tram stop as quickly as possible and then waited. Only a few hours earlier, we had arrived here so full of optimism and excitement. But that feeling was now long gone.

Gone too were the lads we had travelled to the ground with. As we waited for the tram now, we waited alone – as the other Forest fans headed towards their buses, cars or the train station that was nearest to the ground.

We didn't have to wait too long. Within a few minutes our tram arrived. We boarded it, along with just a few other spectators who also queued at our stop.

The tram was already packed, full of smiling, happy Belgians, who were delighted at overturning a two-goal deficit and qualifying for the final.

We pushed our way carefully through them and on to the tram. We made our way through the crowded tram car until we reached the back, where we positioned ourselves for the journey to the station.

Further down the tram a group of Anderlecht fans started singing, and it wasn't long before most of the tram had joined in with them.

I looked all around the tram. I couldn't see another Brit at all. It was just the three of us and a tram full of Anderlecht fans.

At the next stop, more jubilant Belgians got on to the tram – no mean feat as it was already packed. The Anderlecht fans nearest to us pushed closer, as the other passengers moved away from the doors to allow the new passengers onto the tram. They were now almost pressed right against us in the crowded carriage.

They clearly knew that we were Brits. Not just because of the way we dressed, more because we were the only glum-looking supporters on the whole tram.

One of the Anderlecht fans looked straight at us and smiled a smug smile. We attracted a fair few stares and one or two comments were made, but nothing else.

With our backs to the wall of the tram car, we literally rode it out – saying virtually nothing throughout the fifteen-minute journey to the station.

"Just keep together!" I said as we arrived at the Central Station tram stop, and the three of us made our way off the tram.

We then made the short walk into the station, all of us looking around just to check that we weren't being followed. But everything was OK.

We headed for the lockers to reclaim our baggage. With bags in hand, we walked briskly down to the platform, to wait for the train that would take us to catch our ferry.

"Shit!" said Webby, looking at the timetable. "We've got almost half an hour to wait for the train."

There was only a scattering of passengers in the whole of Central Station, with very few of them waiting on the same platform as us. It

14. NUMB

was only 10.30pm, but the place was pretty much deserted. There was nothing else we could do but stand there and wait.

As the minute hand moved very slowly around the station's clock face, it began to feel like a scene from Walter Hill's 1979 film *The Warriors*: the three of us waiting for some gang of Anderlecht fans to come looking for revenge after the night's earlier altercations.

The station clock ticked slowly on. But the only people that did arrive on the platform were a couple more Forest fans, a young lad and his girlfriend – with enough bags to make us think they'd been here for a fortnight!

Eventually our train arrived, and we got on along with just one or two other passengers. The train was already quite full; it had stopped at the station near the ground before reaching Central and then heading towards Ostend.

There was a mixture of Anderlecht and Forest fans on board, with a number of police officers also on the train. We sat down in a carriage of mainly Forest fans. Unsurprisingly, it was subdued and quiet. The mood was as dull and dim as the view from the windows as we moved through the pitch-dark Belgian countryside.

After a while, Till got up and went for a fag. I didn't take that much notice. I just kept staring out of the window into nothingness, still trying to come to terms with our defeat and the manner of it.

Till returned, looking agitated and annoyed.

"Come with me," he said, "I've got some trouble."

As Webby and me got up to see what the problem was, Till explained, "Three Belgians are giving me grief over my hat!"

I'd not noticed until now, but Till was wearing the Anderlecht floppy hat he'd nicked when we were scrapping earlier. It appeared the Belgian lads he'd mentioned had taken offence over his little trophy.

We moved along the train, until we reached where the three Anderlecht lads were stood.

"What's the problem?" asked Till.

They didn't seem to want to make anything more of it once we fronted them, so we rightly let it go. It was something and nothing.

A couple of minutes later we were in Ghent, then onto Brugge. Before too long, we arrived in Ostend.

We made our way through Customs and onto the ferry,

"Find somewhere we can get our heads down," I said to Webby, as we made our way through the decks searching for a quiet and comfortable place to spend the night.

There were several hundred Forest fans on the same crossing, and the mood was no better than the train. The common gripe was that the referee was shit and had all but cost us the match. It was a familiar moan – one that every football fan has heard, and probably used, at some point. But it didn't change anything. We had lost.

I lay down and, using my travel bag as a pillow, I tried to get some kip. We were now into the early hours of Thursday morning, and I was knackered. It all felt such an anticlimax, given the excitement of the past few days. Forest were out and our holiday was almost over. Sleep came quickly enough.

I didn't sleep well. I kept waking throughout the night, but at least I had managed to get some kip. Every time I opened my eyes, Webby seemed to be wide awake. And he was going to be driving us back from London later in the day.

"Get your head down mate," I kept saying, but to no avail.

Till on the other hand slept soundly, no problems at all, out like a light.

It was daylight by the time we had reached Dover harbour. I tried to rouse myself and prepare to get off the ferry.

Again, Webby was already awake. He gave Till a nudge to wake him as well.

14. NUMB

We left the boat as soon as we docked, and boarded the train back to London via a quick trip through Customs.

Webby purchased a newspaper. Once he'd quickly flicked through it, I read it on the train-ride back to London Victoria.

The match report was brief. It mentioned the dodgy penalty, but completely omitted anything regarding our disallowed goal'. Unsurprisingly, it did mention the trouble that occurred before and during the game. Reading the report did nothing to improve my mood, and I quickly turned the pages to read the contents of the rest of the paper.

I dozed off halfway through, only waking when shaken by Webby.

"We're here mate," he said.

The three of us grabbed our bags and left the train, heading for the underground. Forty five minutes later, we were back at Howard and Steve's house. Much to our surprise, DD and Scrawn were already up and waiting.

"Robbed!" said Scrawn, before any of us had a chance to speak. "We watched the highlights last night. Nothing wrong with Hart's goal, and their penalty was a joke!"

"Can't argue with that," I concurred, and we left it there.

We all thanked Steve for his hospitality once more, and climbed into Webby's car for what would be the final leg of our journey. Scrawn was already wearing Till's Anderlecht hat by the time we set off, and he wanted to know all about how Till had managed to get hold of it. Till obliged, taking great delight in reliving the moment, and the five of us went on to swap stories of our encounters since parting the day before.

Despite the stories, and in spite of the best efforts of The Clash and The Jam, I was sound asleep once again as soon as we hit the motorway. I was still completely knackered.

We were back in Nowhere City by dinner, with great credit to Webby for managing to stay awake – given the fact he'd had little or no sleep for over 24 hours.

Our adventure was over. It might not have ended how we wanted it to, but we had still managed to have a great time while it lasted.

That's life!

Footnote

In 1997, Belgian police arrested a group of blackmailers who had extorted several hundred thousand pounds from Anderlecht Football Club.

The blackmailers had threatened to reveal that Anderlecht had paid a bribe to the referee of their UEFA Cup semi-final against Nottingham Forest in 1984.

Although Anderlecht paid substantial amounts to the blackmailers, they continued to demand more money over a ten-year period. Anderlecht were finally forced to bring in the Belgian police to apprehend the blackmailers.

When the truth finally came out, Anderlecht defended their actions – claiming the circa £20,000 they had paid to referee Guruceta Muro had been a 'loan', albeit one that he never actually paid back.

Unfortunately the referee had died in a car accident back in 1987, so he could not be questioned in relation to the incident.

UEFA took action against the Belgian club, but they let Anderlecht off lightly. The club was banned from European competition for just one year as a punishment.

This ban never even took place. Anderlecht successfully appealed it, claiming that the wrong UEFA body had dealt with their case.

Ironically, the match programme from the semi-final included a message printed in English from the Anderlecht chairman, Constant Vanden Stock. It read:

For the officials, players, supporters and fans of Nottingham Forest;
THAT THE BEST BE THE WINNER!

Maybe Vanden Stock should have added – *If not the best... then cheat!!*

After their 'victory' over Forest, Anderlecht went on to play another English team in the final: Tottenham Hotspur.

The first leg of the final took place in Belgium. Again, there was crowd trouble before, during and after the match. The media accused the Belgian police of being heavy-handed towards the English fans, with many Spurs supporters having their buses detained at motorway service stations until just before the game was due to start.

A bar owner shot a Spurs fan dead, in trouble that flared up throughout Brussels prior to the match itself.

The Belgian police had proven ill-prepared to police British football fans, as first Forest and then Spurs supporters were involved in trouble at games in Brussels within the space of a month.

One of the key problems had been their inability to create a robust segregation of fans, both inside and around the grounds.

This point was tragically reinforced a year later at the Heysel stadium in Brussels, when 39 people lost their lives at the European Cup final between Liverpool and Juventus.

Along with the dead, 600 more fans were injured when a wall collapsed as a result of Liverpool fans charging across the terraces – causing widespread panic amongst fleeing Italian supporters.

UEFA responded by banning ALL English teams from ALL European club competitions for five years, with Liverpool serving a further one year.

Since Forest's defeat to Anderlecht in 1984, the Reds' fortunes have somewhat resembled a rollercoaster ride.

They tasted success at Wembley, winning the League Cup in both 1989 and 1990. They also achieved three top-three finishes during the '80's – and always managed to finish inside the top ten right up until Brian Clough's last season in 1992-93, when they were relegated.

Frank Clark won promotion for the team in his first year in charge, and then led Forest to another 3rd place finish the following season, when they were back in the Premiership.

That resulted in Forest returning to Europe – where they reached the quarter-finals before losing to the eventual winners, Bayern Munich.

Clark left as relegation followed in the very next season, 1996-97. This was followed by Forest winning promotion under Dave Bassett at his first attempt.

The yo-yoing continued as Forest succumbed to relegation once more, leaving the Premier League in 1999. They have not returned there as of yet.

In fact Forest dropped into the third tier of English football after the 2004-05 season, for only the second time in their entire history. They spent three miserable seasons there, before winning promotion back to the Championship.

• • •

When the miners went out on strike, at the time of our trip in April 1984, there were still 170 working coal mines operating in the United Kingdom.

The strike lasted far longer than our trip to Brussels. But ultimately it ended in defeat for the miners, and they eventually returned to work on 3rd March 1985, almost a year after it began.

In political terms, this provided Maggie Thatcher with a great victory against what she called 'the enemy within' – not just at the expense of the miners, but at a cost to the whole Trade Union movement.

In July 1984, Thatcher had told the House of Commons:

"We had to fight the enemy without in the Falklands. We always have to be aware of 'the enemy within', which is much more difficult to fight and more dangerous to liberty."

Her conflict with the miners was a controversial one. The police at times took unlawful action to prevent picketing, whilst MI5 was also deployed against the 'subversive' miners.

At Orgreave on 29th May 1984, five thousand striking miners clashed with police, in probably the most violent and memorable scenes of the whole strike.

The day's events were captured on film, and shown repeatedly on BBC news for the next few days. The footage showed the miners throwing all sorts of missiles at the police, and then charging at their lines. Subsequently the police responded with a charge by mounted police to try to restore order.

Only that was not actually how it happened.

The BBC later admitted that the day's events were broadcast in a different order to the way they really happened.

In truth, the miners only resorted to throwing bricks and missiles at the police *after* they had been charged at by mounted officers.

On reflection, Thatcher's talk of 'the enemy within' being a 'danger to liberty' was perhaps a little hypocritical, given the actions of the BBC and the manner in which her government deployed the police and MI5.

Were the miners such a threat to Britain, or were they just fighting to protect their livelihoods?

By 2004, only 11 of those original 170 coalmines were still open in Britain. So perhaps they had every reason to be concerned.

During our trip to watch Forest play Anderlecht, a division was growing between the various coalfield areas. This intensified as pickets from Yorkshire continued to travel down to picket the East Midland pits.

Because of their insistence that a National ballot should take place before going out on strike, the majority of Nottinghamshire and Derbyshire miners eventually formed a breakaway union in December 1984 – the Union of Democratic Mineworkers.

However, some 6,000 out of the 30,000-strong Nottinghamshire miners remained loyal to the NUM. They stayed out on strike for the full length of the dispute.

The bitterness this division caused still exists today, some 30 years on – and the strike is often referenced when Nottingham teams play sporting events against Yorkshire sides.

Shouts of "Scabs!" towards the Nottingham fans are normally met with taunts of "Arthur Scargill, what a wanker!"

Nowadays, more often than not, these sentiments are shouted and sung by folks not old enough to remember what it was really all about.

• • •

I still see all of the main characters involved in the book around today – albeit that we are now a lot older, no wiser, but far better behaved!

Scrawn and DD moved out of Kegworth some time ago, but they both still live locally.

Both are now married with kids – and although I see them regularly, it's never at the football anymore.

Scrawn remains a total sports fanatic, but he's just as keen on Bayern Munich as he is about Forest these days.

DD plays guitar in a local band, and still comes with us to see a few punk gigs from time to time. He's even started attending the odd football match in Nottingham – at Notts County of all places!

Crazy Till is just plain 'Till' these days. He is a completely changed man, who now runs his own business. Also married with children, he still likes a drink or six. But he now prefers to blow his trumpet in a brass band rather than coming along with us to see punk gigs.

Webby remains the quietest one amongst us, but good company never the less. He too still likes a drink, and he has travelled with me to see loads of punk gigs over the past thirty years. We've visited such places as Ireland, Spain, Holland and Germany in the process.

Although I still go to see Forest play, I find that the modern game lacks the level of excitement that football used to have thirty years ago.

Money has become such an integral part of the game that it is no longer a level playing-field, with everything having moved in favour of the so-called 'big clubs'. I'll always follow Forest, but my passion for the game has certainly dimmed.

I still love listening to punk music – and find it a blessing that punk is so far underground that there is no real threat of it being commercialised as football has been.

• • •

As I write this book, I await the start of the 2013-14 football season – which will mark the 30th anniversary of our Anderlecht trip.

Everything that surrounds football has changed so much. Not always for the better.

I hope that the book you have just read gives you a flavour of a time now long gone... the good, the bad and the ugly.